Every Woman Has A Short Story, Men Too!

Short Stories, Poems, Reflections & Quotations

Lillé McGhee-Queen

Copyright © 2004 Lille′ McGhee-Queen

No part of this publication may be reproduced, stored in a retrieval system, or transmitted, in any form or by any means, electronic, mechanical, photocopying, recording, or otherwise, without the written prior permission of the author.

ALL RIGHTS RESERVED.

Cover photo: Sculptured Images Photography
Cover layout: The Design Linc

Produced by:
Jireh Publishing Services
www.jirehpublishing.com

ISBN 1-893995-04-6

TABLE OF CONTENTS

Acknowledgments	5
Forward	7
Introduction	11
Poem, Invisible Influences, Lille' McGhee	13
A Vision to Excel-A Farmer's Daughter Story, Lille' McGhee	15
Reality Quotes 1, Varek Queen	25
Poem, You Help Me to Remember, Linda Garrett	26
Quotes 1, Lille' McGhee	27
Poem, T.G.I.F. (Thanks God, I'm Free), Lille' McGhee	28
Missionary Mary and the Bicycles (A Car Pool Story), Carolyn Jolly Douglas	29
Quotes 2, Lille' McGhee	33
Poem, A Friend Who Supports You, Linda Garrett	34
Reality Quotes 2, Varek Queen	35
Poem, When to Let Go, Lille' McGhee	36
The Singing Artist, Frederico Domondon	38
Poem, Limitless Love, Linda Garrett	45
Quotes 3, Lille' McGhee	46
Poem, Tea on Tuesday, Lille' McGhee	47
Stillness in Vicksburg, Mississippi, Anna Griffin	49
Reality Quotes 3, Varek Queen	53
Poem, You Lift My Spirit, Linda Garrett	54
Quotes 4, Lille' McGhee	55
Poem, Your Radiance Brings Light, Linda Garrett	56
Poem, Pregnant with Child, Lille' McGhee	57
NUZHAT!, Dr. Shehrezard F. Czar	59

Quotes 5, Lille' McGhee	68
Reality Quotes 4, Varek Queen	69
Poem, The Female Sprinter, Lille' McGhee	70
Poem, Feels Like Home, Linda Garrett	73
The Day I Saw the Angels, Carolyn Jolly Douglas	74
Quotes 6, Lille' McGhee	77
An Unfinished Masterpiece, Varek Queen	78
Reality Quotes 5, Varek Queen	81
Poem, Born to Succeed, She Says, Lille' McGhee	82
Poem, My Teacher, Linda Garrett	84
Leaving My Mother's Nest, Angela Stephine Woods	85
Poem, Divine Fortune, Linda Garrett	93
Poem, God's Everywhere, Lille' McGhee	94
Reality Quotes 6, Varek Queen	96
Poem, Hold on to the Vision, Linda Garrett	97
How to Support a Hurting Spouse, Joyce Sherman	98
Quotes 7, Lille' McGhee	108
Poem, No Way to Escape Love, Lille' McGhee	109
Running From, Running To, Carolyn Jolly Douglas	111
Poem, Gifts of an Angel, Linda Garrett	114
Quotes 8, Lille' McGhee	115
Poem, Radiant Spirit, Linda Garrett	116
Poem, The Clock is Ticking, Lille' McGhee	117
Contributors	119
About Author	123

ACKNOWLEDGMENTS

There are so many thanks to give. I hardly know where to begin but—

First, I give thanks to God for giving me the vision to get this book started in January 2004.

Second, I give thanks to my parents, now both deceased, for carving out a spiritual path for me to follow in life, stressing the importance of getting the best education available, maintaining and applying good work ethics, and doing the right thing.

Third, I give thanks to my sisters, and one brother, for sharing their toys, playing games together, helping me with my homework, going fishing with me on Fridays during the summer months, and listening to me practice playing the piano for hours.

Fourth, I give thanks to all of my teachers (elementary and high school), also college professors, who stressed the importance of a good education, the power in education, and education as a key to equal employment opportunities.

Fifth, I give thanks to the ministers and church members at Olive Grove Church in Leasburg, N.C., who encouraged me, as a child, to perform at church plays, recitals, and piano concerts.

Sixth, I give thanks to my husband, Mike Queen, who has loved me during our 34 years of marriage, encouraged me to follow my passion, obtain my career objectives and take risks. Also, who provided great patience whenever I ventured out into various projects (i.e., owning a business, writing books, lecturing, and the art world).

Seventh, I give thanks to our son, Varek Queen, who has provided us with one wonderful, and very talented, grandson, Giano, age 11.

Lille' McGhee-Queen

Eighth, I give Special Thanks to each of the following co-authors who said, "yes" when I asked them to join me in writing this book, *Every Woman Has A Short-Story, Men Too!*

Margaret Williams-Boyd, Dr. Shehrezad F. Czar, Frederico Domondon, Carolyn Douglas, Linda Garrett, Anna Griffin, Varek Queen, Joyce Sherman, Angela Stephine Woods

Ninth, I give Personal Thanks to you (the reader), for purchasing and reading this book. Give it as a gift to others and tell your colleagues, neighbors, relatives and friends to get their personal copies. It is an inspiring book!

Forward

A (Best) Girlfriend's Appreciation Message
by Margaret Williams-Boyd

"My goodness, she knows how to use a typewriter" (a manual one, no less). I could not believe the speed at which she was typing, as I sat and went through my routine of hunt and peck. I finally got up the nerve to ask, "How did you learn to type so fast without even looking at the keys?" Her reply was, "Girl, I don't know."

The year was fall 1960, Person County High School (PCHS) (then a segregated school) located in Roxboro, NC. Just this simple exchange began what became a friendship that continues to this day (2004)! We were in the tenth grade and felt FREE! At PCHS, we weren't the perfect students, nor were we the worst. We were fairly balanced: somewhere between the two extremes. We did some not-so good things; we just didn't get caught. Occasionally, we asked the older guys to give us a cigarette. We would share it and try to inhale the smoke to appear adult-like, but rather we ended up coughing our lungs out. Neither our parents nor teachers were any the wiser of our teenage experiment with cigarettes. Happy were we that they didn't know, for we would have been grounded for weeks! Lille' (Lil) was freer to explore than I was because her parents weren't as strict as mine.

There are lots of miles between Boston, MA, and Elizabeth City, NC. We graduated PCHS in June 1962. Lil's parents sent her to a private school in Boston, while I was sent to Elizabeth City State Teachers College in NC. Notwithstanding the geographical separation, our friendship and loyalty didn't share those miles. E-mail was unheard of, so we remained in touch via U.S.

mail and an occasional phone call. As I write this I'm not sure how we reconnected in D.C. in the mid-60s. As federal government employees, working in the same general area, somehow our paths crossed.

Lil had lots of family there, and I had only a brother, so I spent numerous days and nights at Lil's sister's (Jewel) house. I'll never forget the warm atmosphere of Jewel's home! Sometimes I didn't seem to know how to go home. The comedic conversations (especially Jewel's) and the tasty meals were not to be found in my apartment, so I hung out where the food and camaraderie were to my liking. I didn't pride myself then on being a great cook, and I still don't.

I'm a firm believer that friends are forever. We don't throw away diamonds because they prick our skin. One true friend is not to be weighed against all the jewels of the earth. A good friend is far more precious!

The time would come when once again we would venture away from each other. This time we were really miles apart. In the late 60s and early 70s Lil married, and I feared the worse: loosing my best friend. Not so, it didn't happen! I respected her choice to marry, as well as the privacy she and Glenn deserved (being married to a traveling executive necessitated them relocating periodically). Eventually, they moved to the West Coast, and I remained in D.C. until 1973 when I took residency on the island of San Juan, Puerto Rico, where I would spend the next 4½ years with my husband. "Nothing makes the earth appear so spacious as to have a friend at a distance." True friends will find means of communicating: letters, e-mails, telephones, or by whatever means necessary. In the words of the song writer, "Ain't no mountain high enough…"

Currently, I reside in North Carolina, employed by the county government as a health and medical technician, while Lil resides in Northern California, south of the Francisco Bay. We've shared happy times, sad times (that's what friends are for), parenting skills, as we each have one precious child. We continue to correspond via phone and email several times a week (sometimes a day).

Stop for a moment and try to form a mental image of what life would be like if we didn't have friends: no one to share our most intimate thoughts, no one to pray with, no one to call when we and our mates have a spat. We seem to somehow get by without a lot of life's luxuries, but it's too painful to imagine not having a loyal friend.

One of life's greatest treasures is a true friend, Lil is that treasure!

Kudos for your tenacious loyalty and friendship throughout our 40-plus years!

Best wishes, girlfriend, with your newest book, *Every Woman Has A Short Story, Men Too!*

INTRODUCTION

Every Woman Has A Short Story, Men Too! is a collection of events and experiences in the lives of each writer from culturally-diverse backgrounds, socio-economic levels, education and professions, such as a medical doctor, government employees, artists (painters), pianists, musicians, business owners, law enforcement, homemakers, retired military, landscape architect, storytellers, published authors, single parents, spiritual counselor, and a gaming industry professional. The author and co-authors express their short stories in various forms: a simple quote, poem, and/or a personal story.

The purpose of this book is to allow the reader to think about his or her own personal life story. Also, the seeing, feeling and believing in the importance of getting one's personal story out of their head and capturing it onto printed paper - just like an artist painting on canvas with a paint brush in hand. Stories make history-educational and newsworthy. No one knows your story, nor can they write your story, better than you, the reader of this book. The time is now-this 21st Century-to look at yourself, the economy, and think about the "footnote" that you would like to be remembered by. Whether it's in a poem, a simple quote, or a short story-a long story is okay, too! No one can steal your story but You; that is, if it goes unwritten or untold…

It has been my experience that reading a poem, quote or personal story of another, is like a special healing to me. It often softens my day. Let this book be one of devotion for you, the reader, and a ready reference in times of happiness, sadness and/or joy!

Write your own personal story TODAY—a short or long story. Share it with your friends, family members and the entire world. We are all waiting to read about your life experiences through the printed word.

Invisible Influences
By Lille' McGhee

I have chosen to b'happy,
so priviledged to b'free.

I've chosen to listen to
the silent voice inside of me.

I began to hear that voice
at the tender age of three

No matter where I went,
Or, how fast I ran,
that voice was always there with me.

As a 'frisky' teenage girl,
exploring the many facets of life,
whenever my boyfriend kissed me,
that voice was in the night.

Old college days have come and gone;
I'm enjoying our marital years,

BUT, that voice won't go away,
sometimes I'm happy, other times,
it makes me scared.

At age 59, I suppose,

Lille' McGhee-Queen

that VOICE is here to stay

Is it the voice of God with a message,
OR, my dad's Invisible Influences
still showing me the way?

Thanks, Dad!

A Vision to Excel: A Farmer's Daughter Story
By Lille′ McGhee

I, Lille′ Mc Ghee (aka: Lil), a native of Leasburg, NC, was born into a spiritual family, Mr. Eddie McGhee and Mrs. Mable Mc Ghee, on a cold November day, in the mid-40's. During childhood, I enjoyed a happy home life with one brother, Lysander, and three sisters, Queen, Jewel and Stella. I was labeled "a very forward child" who was always curious about life, music, art, dance and the outdoors. I learned to read before the age of three; was introduced to the family's piano at age four, and by the age of five, a self-taught pianist.

My first public appearance as a pianist occurred at the Olive Grove Baptist Church in Leasburg, NC. I was about five- or six-years old. My grandfather, Rev. Sam Mc Ghee, founded Olive Grove around 1925. I am a member of Olive Grove Baptist Church today and will continue to be a member for the rest of my life.

In elementary and high school years, I played the piano at concerts for various Afro-American church choirs, and an all-girl's rock singing group until I left North Carolina in July 1962.

I enjoyed family activities, community events, and my life on the farm as a happy farmer's daughter (feeding the cows, chickens, pigs, riding mules, planting vegetable gardens, raising tobacco and corn crops).

The most exciting events, with relatives and friends, included going to the movies, in Roxboro and Danville, Virginia (at that time they had an all segregated seating policy), school dances, live plays, dirt-car racing, weekly Friday night fish fry, playing games (i.e., stick ball, softball, board games), and sporting events at school.

From these experiences, I embraced the freedom to run without limits, climb trees, and go fishing on Friday's at my uncle's pond; to think beyond boundaries, develop and apply good sound work ethics. I also took the time to acknowledge opportunities and to daydream about my future outside of the dusty roads, tobacco fields, segregated environments, and to venture off into a major city or town after high school. My parents always encouraged me to be smart, confident, assertive, and an independent thinker and strong leader.

I was an average, to above average student, whenever I took school seriously, in elementary and high school. I attended three segregated public schools in Person County, all located in the Roxboro, North Carolina district. At the age of 14, I graduated from Woodland Elementary in June 1958 and began Person County High School that fall.

Academically, I was an outstanding student in shorthand, typing, general business courses, and especially in law/legal studies. My mom had, unknowingly, prepared me for a future career both in the legal system and law enforcement. As a child, and before entering school, I watched law-related programs such as, Day In Court, Divorce Court, and Perry Mason. My mom even took me with her to the County Courthouse in Roxboro. My parents wanted me to be a lawyer but my vision was to become a criminal court reporter. They stressed education as a means to get ahead in life. I believed them. Many years later in my professional career, I became a Criminal Court Reporter.

At high school, I tried out for the Girl's Basketball Team-I didn't make the cut. But, that did not greatly affect me because there were ways to support my home team by attending evening basketball games against other local schools. I never sought out nor desired to be that perfect child but rather, to enjoy high school life, occasionally make Honor Roll, and socialize with my friends. On one occasion (out of four years of high school), I recalled skipping class-the night of the Senior Prom. On a few occasions, my girlfriends and I shared cigarettes. Fortunately, neither my parents nor teachers found out what we were up to. I would have been grounded and disciplined by my parents for WEEKS! We were just fooling around and trying to act like young adults.

I graduated from Person County High School in June 1962. In July 1962, I caught the midnight train from Danville, VA to Boston, MA leaving the people I loved most behind: my parents, sister, brother, and high school boyfriend. They waved good bye as the train took off in the night.

My parents wanted me to continue my education beyond high school. They had saved enough money for me to enroll in a private school, Hickox Secretarial in Boston, MA. What a beautiful view! This was my first exposure to integrated education. I was a southern girl who "talked funny" or rather "differently" than my Boston-born classmates. It did not matter a lot because I knew my purpose in school and for being in Boston-that was to excel academically! I did. I took all of my courses seriously, and at age 17, felt like I was growing up into a young lady. I wanted to make my family feel very proud. They were very pleased. Very proud! I was too!

In winter of 1964, I began a career with the Federal Government in Washington, DC. I was a GS-3 Level, Clerk Typist. I felt very happy and pleased to be residing in DC (since childhood, I vacationed in DC almost every summer and stayed with relatives. I was thrilled by all of the tall Federal Buildings and imagined that one day I would be working for the Federal Government). I worked full-time and went to college evenings, part-time, to advance my career. I was then promoted to a GS-4, Clerk Stenographer, GS-5, Secretary and GS-6, Secretary-Stenographer.

I was very pleased, and also my parents, to see my career advancement in the Federal Government. My career was in motion; however, I wanted more. Much more! To get more, it was necessary that I push myself in the direction of my vision. It was up to me to excel through quality education and outstanding job performance. I wanted to get into a para-professional position within the Government or venture out into private industry.

After studying Court and Conference Reporting for nearly three years (both full time and part time), I graduated with an Associate of Arts Degree from Strayer College, Washington, DC in the summer of 1972. I became a Freelance Court Reporter, which involved taking depositions, conferences, and courtroom proceedings at Criminal Courts, both at the Arlington Circuit Court, in Arlington, VA, and the Alexandria Circuit Court, in Alexandria, VA. Court reporting is a very challenging profession, which required maximum concentration at all times. I learned quite a bit about the criminal justice system and was able to transfer that knowledge into future careers.

During the time that I was building my career, I took time out for marriage (May 1969) to my "one and only" husband, Glenn. He was a student at the University of Maryland, College Park, MD. In January 1971, we had our son, Varek, who's an only child.

We relocated to Southern California in summer of 1974. We drove across country, 3,000 miles, in a yellow Vega. It was very tiny. Our son slept in the backseat. We traveled across country during the day and stayed at a hotel in the evening. We barely made it to California-our car ran hot as we were crossing the Arizona desert. We took our time in getting to California-it took us about five days. What a vacation!

We had never been to the West Coast. This was our first time in California, and driving on a California freeway was totally overwhelming. My foot felt like it was jumping off the pedal as we pulled into Los Angeles. Shortly after we arrived, everything seemed to fall into place. We stayed in different hotels for several weeks, and after three months purchased our first home. It was a single story three-bedroom house with a very big fenced-in backyard. We lived in Carson, California (Los Angeles County). We had friendly neighbors. It was a very lovely community! We felt safe-our next-door neighbor was a Los Angeles Police. We enrolled our son into a private school and I began to job hunt.

Initially, I was unsuccessful in getting back into the Federal Government in Los Angeles. So, in the interim, I worked as a legal secretary in a Law Firm on Wilshire Boulevard. I maintained my court-reporting skills speed by taking dictation on my court-reporting machine from my boss-a very nice attorney. I also practiced on my own, one or two hours nightly, because I knew that at some point, I would receive a call from a Federal agency asking me to come in for a job interview and I wanted to be ready whenever that telephone rang. It happened! One day, the phone rang-I answered. That was the call that I had been waiting for…

In 1976, the Personnel Manager of the U.S. Department of Justice, Immigration and Naturalization Service in Los Angeles called me in for a job interview. I was interviewed by the Senior Immigration Judge. I was unsure how the interview went because I could not read the Judge-I even felt somewhat intimidated by him. He had a very deep voice and did not smile. I was later offered the open Court Reporter's position and reinstated into the Federal Service. I began employment with Immigration. My job title was, "Official Court Reporter." I prayed to God with words of thanks. I was once again in a para-professional position as a Court Reporter.

While I was experiencing job security and feeling very grateful to be employed by Immigration, I quickly realized that my career advancement was unlikely to happen in the Court Reporting field. I looked at my options; continued my education at LA Harbor College and at the same time tried out my writing skills.

During 1978, I wrote, and self-published my first book, Handbook of Procedures for the Immigration Courtroom. It was recognized and accepted by Immigration. It felt wonderful seeing my book in the Immigration Trial Attorneys' Library. The entire time that I was writing the book, I received a lot of support from the Immigration Judges, Immigration Trial Attorneys, Immigration Defense Attorneys, Immigration personnel, and friends and family. The book was a complete success, both personally and financially. It was at that point that I picked up a new set of skills- selling and marketing my book at legal tradeshows, conferences and seminars!

There was a thirst for more education and for a more clearly defined Federal professional position with career growth opportunities. To start this process, I became enrolled in an accelerated undergraduate program, "Human Resources and Organizational Behavior", at the University of San Francisco (Los Angeles).

In 1982, I received a Bachelor of Science Degree from the University of San Francisco; was interviewed for a position as Special Agent, U.S. Department of Defense, Defense Investigative Service, Washington, DC, and relocated, with family, back to the Washington, DC area in (Maryland), fall 1982. My career advanced to a GS-11 within a few years. I simply enjoyed the status of being a Special Agent; conducing security clearance background investigations at all levels, including the White House, the Senate, and Congressional personnel in DC.

Our son, Varek, attended junior and high school in Maryland. He graduated from high school in 1989 and went directly into the U.S. Army. Glenn and I decided to look at our career options and return to the West Coast. We selected Northern California and then decided upon Milpitas as our first choice to reside. Both of us had firm job offers before actually leaving the

East Coast. We even had an opportunity to purchase a home in Milpitas, before physically moving back to California. I transferred to The Office of Personnel Management, Office of Federal Investigations in Menlo Park, CA, with Headquarters in San Francisco.

Glenn accepted an executive's position with a major book publishing company in Mountain View, CA. My status as a Senior Federal Investigator went unchanged through 1996. Due to the Federal Government's downsizing and privatizing, changes occurred in the Investigation's Division, Office of Personnel Management. Some investigators lost their jobs. I, along with some other Federal Investigators, was fortunate enough to maintain employment. We transferred into a privately owned investigative company that had Federal Contracts. There was a strong need for experienced Federal Investigators.

In 1997, I began to have a lot of difficulty with using my hands-constant pains. I was diagnosed with tendonitis of the hands. I could see that the condition of my hands would ultimately interrupt my long career as a Senior Investigator that began in 1982. It was just a matter of time before I turned in my badge and walked away. It happened! I was placed on permanent disability in 2001 and said, "Good bye" to a successful career in Law Enforcement.

LET'S TURN THE CLOCK BACK - I AM THINKING OF MY PARENTS...

My mother and dad were supportive to me in most of the choices that I made in life, especially career and education. My dad died on July 24, 1986, due to cancer of the throat. My mother died of an unexpected "massive" heart attack on August 13, 1990. When my father died, my mom helped me through my long period of grief-when mom died, dad was not present to help me go through the grieving process.

August of 1990 began the onset of difficult times for me. Our son was away in the military, my husband was at the height of his career, I was a new investigator in Silicon Valley, and we had no immediate family on the West Coast. I felt sad and needed a distraction in my life.

I, once again, attempted to challenge my grief by acquiring more education, a Master's Degree. I enrolled in a graduate program, Human Relations and Organizational Management, University of San Francisco in March 1991. My mom was still the only "one" thing on my mind-so I could not FULLY concentrate on the school requirements. After nearly a year or so into the two-year program, I walked away. I had to discover other ways to challenge my grief. I developed personal fun hobbies like designing scarves and teaching classes on *How to Wear & Tie Scarves*. I participated in modeling shows and met new friends outside of the work environment. I also became more focused on my duties as an Investigator.

GETTING BACK ON TRACK…

October 2001, one month after "9/11", I became the CEO & President of Artistic Gift Baskets in Silicon Valley, San Jose, CA, through December 2003. Due to the economy downturn in Silicon Valley, I expanded my company's products and services beyond gift baskets by organizing and conducting *sell out* business seminars and workshops. I also founded two organizations in 2002−the BM&W (Business Men & Women) Networking Club and the Wise Women's Tea Club. Times were getting tight, business wise in the Valley, and it was necessary to expand to survive in business!

IT'S NOW MARCH 2004. . .

It is time to take a look at my past, present and future life. I am having lots of fun! I am partially retired, enjoying various projects and living an almost stress-free life. The pace is must slower. The air is fresher. I can enjoy my husband's, "Paradise Garden", each morning in the backyard. The greatest joy in my life includes spending time with our eleven-year-old grandson, Giano. Giano and I are both much alike-we are both artists, enjoy playing tennis, soccer, climbing trees, visiting art galleries and museums. Giano and I take time out to write short stories, poems and quotes.

There is nothing that I desire to change at this point about ANY aspects of my life's choices: careers, educational/financial accomplishments, family members, in-laws, nor my spouse. On second thought, my *Afro* is changing to a lighter color. It was once totally black! What happened? I guess nothing remains the same. My life has been wonderful and continues to be filled with adventure, high energy and excitement. I work out almost daily.

Thanks, mom and dad, for the great spiritual guidance and strong work ethics that you taught me, by example. You taught me to obey and respect "The Golden Rules", and pointed my feet in the best direction. Just like everyone who is reading this book, I continue to experience both the "highs" and "lows" in life-that is part of the journey. My life's experiences include the "good" and "bad" choices I've made in relationships, employment, and career choices that were not mentioned in this book. But, overall, I have come through in good shape.

There are no permanent scars in my life. I am grateful for what I have at this moment—at age 59! My single objective now is to get this book, *Every Woman Has A Short Story, Men Too*!, published before my 60th birthday in late November of 2004. Everybody has a short story-most of us have very long stories, poems, quotes, and testimonials to share with the WORLD. Take some time out right now! Put your thoughts into words, your visions into action and ideas onto paper. Why should you leave this Universe with an untold story? So, tell your short story TODAY! Others may grow from your experiences.

"I WILL NOT DIE AND LEAVE THIS WONDERFUL WORLD WITHOUT A FOOTNOTE."

Reality Quotes #1
By Varek Queen

"A woman is only as faithful as her options."

"If you are mixed up in something, make sure you are at the top!"

"If shadows could talk, there would be no silence."

You Help Me to Remember
By Linda Garrett

You help me to remember
To believe in myself
Despite obstacles or setbacks
To have faith in my own power
And that I already know all the answers
You remind me that looking inside myself
Will create more clarity in my life
That I am responsible for creating my own destiny
And for choosing my perceptions of events
You help me to remember
That being true to myself
Is always the best path to follow
Most of all, you remind me
That the loving and giving of friendship
Is what living life is all about

Quotes 1
By Lille' McGhee

"It is in darkness that character is formed, but through daylight upon which it's measured, evaluated, and discussed."

"A visionary, like an artist, can see far beyond an unfinished painting."

"Look beyond the obvious in search of the real truth!"

T.G.I.F.
(Thanks God, I'm Free)
By Lille' McGhee

Every woman has a short story
Every woman wants a cup of tea
Every woman is reaching beyond
Tomorrow,
BECAUSE,
Every woman wants to
BE FREE!
A freedom to love
A freedom to live
A freedom to cry
A freedom to give
A freedom to run
A freedom to play
A freedom to control
What happens to her today
THANKS GOD, I'M FREE!

Missionary Mary and the Bicycles
(A Car Pool Story)
By Carolyn Jolly Douglas

Riding in car pools can be an enlightening experience. I have met some very interesting people in my car pool and have received some valuable insights on how we live an interconnected existence. Let me share my encounter with Missionary Mary.

Every morning as I dress for work, I say a prayer for the car pool, giving thanks for the drivers and the riders. My desire is to pull up to the designated spot, have a couple of people hop into the car, and zip off to the city. My ulterior motive is to get into San Francisco without being caught up in early morning traffic.

One fateful morning, I arrived at the car pool area to find no riders waiting. Two vehicles, a car and a truck, were ahead of me. This meant I could possibly be late getting to my office, so I immediately rattled off a prayer, giving thanks for enough people to fill the vehicles ahead of my car and mine as well. Every few minutes, I'd look into the rearview mirror to see if some riders were making their way to the stop. After about ten minutes of anxiously waiting, I noticed a small group of four people with two bicycles slowly walking towards the stop. It was apparent that these riders, two women and two men, knew one another and had a common lifestyle.

They were distinctively dressed, quite unlike the young people of today. There were no tattoos, visible body piercing, exposed midsections, or unique hairstyles. Their clothing caused me to think of the Amish or Mennonites whose style of dress immediately identifies them as being separate from the mainstream population. It is intended to be an expression of humility and their faith. The men wore brimmed hats, suit coats with vests, and well-worn shoes. The women wore simple light colored long dresses with long sleeves; their long hair was contained in a cap, which only covered a part of the head. They wore no makeup, not even the basic colorless foundation. I just knew they had to be a religious sect, but I did not know which one.

Before entering the waiting vehicles, they embraced each other and said their good wishes for each other's day. The young men got into the first car and were whisked off to the city. The small truck ahead of me had only enough room for just one other person. And, there was no way I could carry the two young women with their bicycles in my little Nissan. The young women immediately began negotiating how to get to San Francisco. One of the young women asked the female truck driver if she would allow them to put their bicycles in the truck bed. Once permission was given, the other young woman asked if she could ride with me. Of course, I replied yes. She got into the front passenger seat, but we needed another rider to meet the minimum number of three for the carpool lane. Just as I was about to point this out, the back door of my car opened, and a gentleman quietly slid onto the back seat and off we went to the city.

Usually driving is contemplation time for me. This is the time when I focus my thoughts and make decisions on how my day will unfold. But today, I was intrigued. Who were these people? Why did they dress in that way? Were they a cult? What message were they trying to convey? Just, who were they? My curiosity got the best of me so I began a conversation by posing a few questions, and hoped I would get the answers I was seeking.

The young woman, I will call Mary, told me that they were followers of Christ and they had taken a vow to live their lives just as Jesus and the disciples had lived. They were missionaries. That meant they did not have a permanent roof over their heads and sometimes slept under the stars. Their primary function was to spread the word of love and they take their lead or guidance from the words in the New Testament of the Bible. So, when they go out into the world to spread their message, they go two by two.

Next, I inquired about her style of dress and Mary shared the story of her past history. Before becoming a missionary, she had been of the Gothic culture and dressed in that dark style. Her life was filled with a lot of darkness. She had use drugs, lived on the streets, was promiscuous, and basically had no regard for life or living. One day she found herself so depressed about her life that she thought of committing suicide. In fact, she was ready to end her life when a strange young man came up to her and started telling her about how he changed his life and that she could do the same. They spent the next few hours talking together. Mary believed his primary purpose was to keep her alive. When she insisted that it was time for her to go, he elicited a promise from her to meet him again on the next day. And she replied that if she made it through the night she would meet him in the park again.

To make a long story shorter, she took the messages of life that he gave her seriously and began the deliberate process of changing her life. And in doing so, she felt it was necessary to dress and conduct herself completely opposite of the Gothic culture. That meant dressing in a way that showed humility and separation from the world.

As we neared the drop off point in San Francisco, I asked, "Where are you going today?" She broke out in a big smile and said, "Oh, we are on our way to Golden Gate Park and the Haight to look for young people who may be ready to change their lives for the better." She said she wanted to return what was given to her by helping someone else. As she began to exit the car, she turned and said, "Thank you for helping me get this far." The gentleman who had sat quietly in the backseat finally spoke, "How will you get to the park?" To which she replied, "Christ will make a way, and that is why they had their bicycles." If necessary they would cycle to the park. Then he hurriedly asked one more question as he was getting out of the car, "What about food? Do you have some food?" She said, "No." He reached into his pocket, handed her some money without looking to see how much he was giving, and then bound off toward his job. She smiled and said, "Bless you." Pocketing the money, she went off to assist her traveling companion who was removing their bicycles from the truck bed.

As I proceeded up the street to the parking garage, my thoughts went to how we three people, basically strangers to one another, came together in support of one another. I needed riders to have access to the car pool lane. My riders needed to get into the city. Mary needed her daily needs met. And my gentleman passenger was afforded the opportunity to supply Mary with loaves and fishes for the day. Perhaps, like Mary, he too, was giving back to life. Who said the gift had to be monumental? And, I got the opportunity to witness it first hand.

Was our shared experience coincidence, synchronicity, or a divine intelligence orchestrating our lives? You can decide for yourself. But whatever it is called, on that day I experienced a moment of clarity on how the Spirit shows up in our daily lives. It operates through each person in our ordinary doings.

The evidence was squarely before me that we truly are helpers, one to another. I am convinced that as we open our eyes to see divine activity right where we are, right in the moment of what we are doing, then Life shows us how its interplay supports all of us, and that we are connected to one another in some way. As in this case, maybe all that is required of any person is that we show up and be open to the possibility of something good happening. For when we open to the experience of life, amazing things can and do happen.

Quotes 2
By Lille' McGhee

"Positive environments invite energy and creativity-negative environments drain intellectual growth and stimulation."

"A confident leader is an outstanding follower! Become a leader…"

"To exhale is the first sign of wanting to be free!"

A Friend Who Supports You
By Linda Garrett

A friend who supports you is someone who…
Believes in you when no one else seems to
Is there for you whenever you need them
Accepts you the way you are, regardless of what you do
Understands that where you are on your path is exactly where you need to be
Supports you through the toughest times
Acknowledges your strength and your power
Inspires and uplifts you and loves you no matter what
Teaches you to be a friend to yourself
Allows you to express and feel your feelings in a way that is healing
Gives you encouragement when you need it most
Helps you to grow in ways that support your courage and confidence
Makes you realize that love and friendship are what living life is all about
A friend who supports you is an incredible and precious gift
Thank you for being that friend to me

Reality Quotes #2
By Varek Queen

MESSAGE TO FUTURE WIFE…
"To you, my wife…I love you and no other."

"Good or bad, there's nothing in the world that a little boy would not do in order to have a dad."

"Never think that your children are smart despite of you—it's because of you!"

When to Let Go…
By Lille' McGhee

Our parents, our friends say,
"Hold onto life's circumstances
until the very end."

Sometime it's a relationship,
a business venture,
and other times,
a best friend.

Just think of the hours,
the stress, the pain,
all of this is likely
to cause

Wake up, get a grip,
'cause you're the person
HERE in charge.

There comes a crossroad,
a moment of uncertainty in life,
about what is best to do
Take ONE moment,
look inside yourself,
then ask God to see
you through.

Every Woman Has a Short Story, Men Too!

Don't hestitate, to give up,
AND get out of,
circumstances that
no longer add value;

That's the only way to
regain self-respect,
dignity,
and to restore
personal power.

All things are
not meant to be,
my friend,
so, look at the flashing
red signs

Detach from your emotions,
Just take that FIRST step,
a SECOND step,
and move ahead of the line.

In life, when it does not grow,
Just "Let It Go!"
"LET IT GO!"

G-O-N-E!

The Singing Artist
By Frederico Domondon

As a child, Frederico Domondon's world was always dominated by the arts. Growing up as a homebody in the Manila suburbs, he spent most of his time drawing beautiful female faces. He discovered his talent in art at the age of seven and has never stopped sketching. Little did he know that some day he would be an artist.

Music was very important to his family. His mother, a professional and excellent pianist, required everyone in the family to take piano lessons. After a few lessons, Frederico discovered that he could play the piano by ear. This was no surprise since his mother did the same thing. While attending grade school, he was active in school choirs. He learned early that he could sing in tune and possessed perfect rhythm. Of all the siblings who took piano lessons, he was the gifted one who retained the interest, and obviously, inherited his mother's talent and love for music.

During the seventies, the music industry in Manila at that time was huge and the influence of American music very strong. Frederico sang and played songs of American pop stars, such as the Carpenters and The Bee Gees to name a few. At the age of 15, he dreamt of becoming a recording star. But as he packed his suitcase and migrated to the United States the next year, the dream diminished. His mother was marrying a wealthy American lawyer, whom she had met during a performance and fell in love. He adopted the children and brought them to the U.S. where Frederico's passion for art and music were put aside as he pursued an accounting degree at his mother's counsel.

Every Woman Has a Short Story, Men Too!

After graduating from school and working as an accountant for a year, his art began to haunt him. He was heavily inspired by the beauty and vibrancy of San Francisco, where he currently resided. The Impressionist masters, Monet, Matisse and Van Gogh were his inspirations when he decided to hit the canvasses once more. While his love for art was his main focus, his interest in music crumbled when he sold his piano. (The piano was taking up too much space in his studio, which was filled with acrylic paints blank white canvasses.)

As an artist, Frederico was prolific and produced as much as a hundred paintings a year, even with a full-time job. He spent his sleepless nights painting in the wee hours of the morning. His day job was dull and his art served as a release away from the office. His work started selling immediately to his friends who saw the potential in the budding young artist. They could not resist his bold and colorful renditions of Monet's Water Lilies or Van Gogh's Sunflowers.

In 1994, his first break as an artist came when he was offered a private exhibition in a beautiful home in Atherton, CA where a dozen of his paintings sold. Other juicy offers to exhibit in the city's cafes and street fairs started pouring in. His impressionistic work with its vibrant colors appealed to the emotions of the curious art buyers. Calls started coming in from young art lovers who wanted a piece of his collection. Out-of-state clients who stumbled on his website flew from New York and Arizona to buy from him. All of a sudden, he was in demand and was on top of the world.

He learned that most art buyers bought his art impulsively. "It was an emotional purchase," he said back then. Pricing and selling his work came easy for him: he named his price and they paid it. Not only was his work stunning and extraordinary, his patrons felt his warmth as a person and passion as an artist. A sociable person, Frederico, often took his clients to dinner and visited with them. "My paintings are like my children. My patrons become a part of my life and I become a part their lives too. I often asked for custody to visit my paintings," he answered when asked how he feels about selling his work. Several of his patrons have kept in touch with him throughout the years. How could they forget him with his paintings hanging on the walls in their private homes? His collectors always felt Frederico's presence.

    The possibility of making a living as an artist began to hit him. There is only one thing missing: a studio with enough space to hold his ever-increasing inventory of original paintings. He thought that living in a small one-bedroom apartment would be uncomfortable while painting full time. One day, his mother advised him to look around for a home in the suburbs. While scouting for homes in Vallejo, CA, he fell in love with a four bedroom, two-story Mediterranean style home. It was a perfect nest for an artist. It had plenty of windows to bring adequate lighting and its 2,000 square foot space would serve as a very comfortable working area to paint. The arches in front of the home reminded him of one of his paintings. But there was a financial problem: he did not have enough money for a down payment. Lady luck was on his side when, out of the blue, he sold several original works. Within three weeks, he made an offer and moved in sooner than he thought. Not only did he surprise himself, but he also surprised his friends who always thought of him as a happy go lucky artist who suddenly, became a homeowner.

    In 1999, just within a few months of buying the home, he surprised everyone again when he quit his day job. Being a full-time artist was his next challenge, especially with the monthly mortgage payment. Frederico thought of a strategy to make his new life work. With the advice of a friend, he joined a networking club where he gained immense exposure, selling a dozen original paintings to a few of its members. A series of profitable Open Studios were held in his home. Fine wine and dinner would be served during this event, which helped to sell the artwork. He also actively participated and sold his paintings in Northern California's street fairs from spring to fall year after year.

He always knew that selling his work would not be a problem since sales were coming in steadily. Coming from a family background of politicians and businessmen, he was a charmer and a great salesman. He loved his work, and his patrons often felt that.

Other artistic accolades came in after. In the year 2000, he made the list of one of the world's best artists through an Internet poll. Often acting as a consultant to aspiring artists and because of his marketing genius, they recognized him as a role model. In ten years, Frederico had sold over 1,000s of his own paintings and made a comfortable living out of it.

Destiny took its turn, when in January of 2003, while exhibiting his work in an upscale restaurant, he was accidentally hired as a pianist. It occurred during dinnertime when his friends asked him to play the piano. The restaurant owner, an art lover himself, fell in love with Frederico's piano music and offered him the job on the spot, which due to the numerous years of not practicing, he nervously accepted. Surprisingly, his talent in playing the piano came back and he could play almost every song anyone requested. Not only was the restaurant adorned with his attractive paintings, but it was also filled with the soothing sound of his piano playing. The servers started to joyfully hum to Frederico's tunes while waiting on their customers, which cheered up the diners.

Then, Frederico started to sing. "People expect you to sing if you play the piano and my mother always told me that I could sing. After years of not singing, I started singing again. All of a sudden, I'm belting out romantic ballads in front of everybody in this fancy restaurant. I have never dreamt that I would do what my mother did for a living. I have never imagined performing with a tip jar right in front of me. At 38 years old, I'm having the time of my life," he said.

Another break came that same year when he was a last minute hired by his mother to temporarily replace the lead singer (who called in sick) in her own band. His job (well done) was to sing a dozen ballroom type songs in a five-star restaurant with only a few days of practice. Although that experience was nerve wrecking, it was fulfilling to Frederico as he sang and danced courageously on stage in front of 500 strangers. Just like a celebrity, fans approached him after the performance and asked him questions, such as "are you a recording star?" He humbly answered, "thanks for the complement but I'm not. This is actually my first gig on stage", which surprised the inquirers. The event boosted Frederico's confidence as a performer. On New Year's Eve, he was hired to perform solo in the same fancy restaurant. Both performances received excellent reviews and had placed his vocals talents on the professional level.

Frederico always knew that he had a good speaking and singing voice. A few years back, he made a phone call to a radio station to request a song and was offered a disc jockey job. He once phoned a female clientele and when her husband answered the call, he suspiciously thought that Frederico had personal intentions towards his wife. Later, the husband apologized and explained to Frederico that it was "his sexy and deep voice" that caused him to be suspicious. A big laugh came out of it. He also became the president of the networking club he joined, and he was always complemented as a great speaker and leader.

His listeners often told him that his sultry voice was reminiscent of Johnny Mathis. On the other hand, other musicians always complemented him on his unique and soothing tone. "Being self-trained in my painting, singing, and playing the piano, it is practice that makes it perfect. My goal as a singer is to hit all the right notes and keys, and to be very comfortable in performing in front of an audience. Singing, like my painting, is my passion and I would like to have fun doing it. After a year of singing, I have improved a lot and I am confident of my ability to perform in front of people. What makes me happy is when people feel my emotion and passion when I'm singing, just like the way they feel with my paintings," he said.

Armed with a unique voice and a magical stage presence, Frederico's tip jar gets filled up quickly during every performance. Not only that, he also gets compensated very well for any private gigs he is hired to perform. "I was hired recently to perform at a private party and they doubled my asking fee. I was ecstatic when they handed me the check. I have not treated singing as a job yet-to me it is just a hobby," he said in January of 2004.

However, Frederico's perception of his future in music had recently changed. His new dream is to produce and market his own CDs and DVDs with his beautiful paintings on the covers. Hopefully, he wished that someday, a major recording studio would recognize his musical talent. He is currently in the process of developing his first CD, to be released in the fall of 2004. Don McLean's 70s hit, Vincent (Starry Starry Night), his favorite song, will be featured. Vincent Van Gogh is his favorite artist and this song inspired him to sing. "Recording my first CD is as exciting as creating an original painting. It is a labor of love. I can't wait to share it with everyone," he excitedly declared.

Performing weekly in an elegant restaurant has helped Frederico develop a growing fan base that cannot wait to purchase his first CD. Several fans are starting to order the CD ahead of time. This is very inspiring to him. "I am very positive about this upcoming project. The universe is telling me to sing and as long as everybody is loving it, I will never stop singing," he said with a big smile.

What about the paintings? "I will never give up on my paintings, though. It is still the one that pays my bills. I'm planning a trip to Tuscany this summer, to get inspired again," he answered. "Although someday, I want to be recognized for both my talents-music and art," he proudly stated. So, will Frederico

Domondon's crooning bring him as much success as an artist did? "As long as I put my heart and soul in my work, I know it will be successful. I'm already feeling it at this moment. You will never know, until you try," he concluded. As they say, "dreams do come true." Looking back at the singing artist's history, his dream has a good chance of becoming real.

Limitless Love
By Linda Garrett

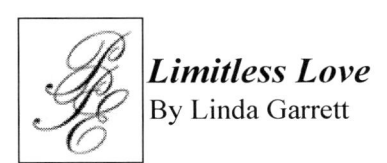

When you awaken to the truth of your soul
The warmth of the light overflows throughout your being
It is a journey no one else has traveled
You are, and always will be, a unique gift to the world
To realize the power within you
Allows the creation of miracles
Welcome the love of the divine into your heart
And know with certainty that you can, and very soon will
Create what it is your heart and soul desires
To help other people and enjoy what we do
Is our priceless purpose
More valuable than any amount of gold or diamonds
It is the true clarity of the sacred love within
We are all here to discover
The incredible creative power that we all came here with
And the limitless love each of us are here to remember

Quotes 3
By Lille' McGhee

"People who care MOST about you will PUSH you forward-all others, simply PUSH!"

"I will not die without a legacy, or at minimum, a footnote."

"Sustained personal motivation comes from within and not from the outside."

Tea on Tuesday
(Mom, A Girl's Best Friend)
By Lille' McGhee

I would give a million bucks,
to have my MOM alive
with me today

MOM was a strong woman
of spirit

She taught me everything I know,

She taught me how to pray.

Without MOM,
I would have taken
a completely different path;

But, MOM held my hand,
Made me feel very
special
Those feelings today still last.

When I look into Heaven's skies,
I know my MOM is always
looking down

She's holding dad's

hand now,
Their love is so profound.
MOM'S favorite day
was TUESDAY
'Cause
she and her girlfriends
all gathered around

They sat near the
Wooden 'pot-belly' stove,
dipped snuff,
told girlee jokes,
quilted winter quilts,
drank cups of tea,
until the sun went down.

Like MOM,
My favorite day is
TUESDAY

My girlfriends and
I meet for a spot of tea,
BUT,
our conversations
are so inspiring,
a ONE-HOUR lunch
break, very often EXPANDS
to Three!

"GIRLFRIEND, PASS THE POT OF TEA…"

Stillness In Vicksburg, Mississippi
By Anna Griffin

There are times at night, and even now, when I awake from sleep for no particular reason. When that happens, sometimes I go back to sleep without hesitation but other times, I toss and turn-I can't seem to resume that peaceful state of sleep. At those moments my mind begins to reflect on some of the happy events, sad occasions, or unpleasant situations I have encountered in my life. Sometimes, I think about the events of the day while driving down a California freeway at 70 miles per hour. This is especially so when, all of a sudden, traffic slows down to a complete stop. Now, I am trapped—I mean-sitting still in my car. I can't move—can't go anywhere. I feel stuck until I remember that my cell phone is in my purse right beside me. I take it out and start to call people whom I haven't spoken to in a long while. Now, I am beginning to feel much better.

    Or, I might think about the job interview I had the day before and now wonder why I couldn't just sit still and wait until my name was called. There was a water fountain in the lobby nearby where I was sitting. All of a sudden (perhaps nerves), I was so thirsty. I thought I would die if I didn't get up and get a drink. After that, I had to go to the little girl's room. When I returned to the lobby, the receptionist finally called my name. I was escorted into the interview room. At points during the interview, I felt myself fidgeting in my chair just like a schoolgirl. It felt like I was still the young girl back in Mississippi, in the 50's and 60's, when my mother made sure my brothers and I got properly dressed for church on Sunday.

During this era, there was a time when certain clothes were considered Church clothes and all others were for play or school. My mother always made sure we had on our "Sunday" clothes before she would put on her clothes. It took her longer to get dressed than the four of us. So, once we were all properly dressed, we asked mom's permission to wait for her outside on the front porch. She agreed. We all cautiously marched outside but we didn't stay on the porch very long before the yard wooed us away. Needless to say, we got our *Sunday* clothes dirty. (Most of the yards in the South had very little, if at all, green grass-mostly dirt and dust.) When mom came out of the house and saw the dirt on our clothes, she exclaimed, "Get in this house right now, and change your clothes, so we can go to church!" We didn't make it to church on time that Sunday, and our mom never forgot the incident.

The routine of mom making sure we had on our own clothes first and hers second never changed, but we realized that asking her to go outside to wait on the porch would never happen again. Instead, mom developed a different way for us to wait. After we were dressed, she would say, "Look at me, and hear what I say. I want you all to sit on this couch, and sit still! Don't move until I'm ready to go." Of course, we couldn't sit still, so we moved around and played on the couch and when we heard mother's footsteps coming toward us, we quickly sat still, and mom was pleased because she liked it when we were clean and still.

Thinking about my childhood calms my spirit. I relax and return to sleep. When I awake several hours later, I feel in tune with the quietness that surrounds me. I listen to the various sounds of my apartment: the heater going off and on, the cracking of the house, footsteps upstairs, a toilet flushing, people talking. As I listen, I remember something I forgot to do before going to bed and I get up and take care of it. When I get back in bed, I listen to the cars driving up and down the street and hear the people walking and talking. It is a warm night and the rhythm around me lulls me back to the summers of my childhood in Vicksburg, Mississippi.

Each year when summer rolled around, mom made sure that she had her fishing poles and bait (worms and minnows) ready for her daily fishing expedition. She'd leave very early morning-every day except Saturday and Sunday of course-and return around noon. It was a peaceful and joyous occasion for her to sit still on the banks of the Bayou in total solitude. It didn't really matter whether she caught any fish or not because she always returned, relaxed and refreshed. She radiated with incredible smiles-very big and peaceful smiles! Mom also handed out big hugs and kisses to each of us. Even as young children, we knew that there was something in the stillness of the water that renewed her spirit and exhaled the worries of the day.

Outdoor sports were a way of life for my parents. My dad's favorite Fall sport was game hunting. I can vividly recall the enthusiasm in the air when he began to prepare for a hunting excursion. He started preparing the night before by gathering the things he needed for the trip. Dad displayed very open smiles while telling us that he would be gone all day and would return home late. He also said, "Be good and help your mom with chores during the day." I begin to wonder if he was secretively glad to get away from us kids for a little while, but reconsidered, "No, that was not the case." This was one of the ways that dad expressed his happy childhood memories.

As young children, we weren't sure exactly when dad returned home from one of his expeditions, except that it was dark. We always associated darkness with being very late. When the door opened, he stood tall in the doorway, smiling with dead birds (quail) held proudly in his hands. I was frightened and wouldn't go near him. My brothers were excited, of course, and took the birds and examined them before cleaning them. Then dad would tell us about his game hunting experience. I immediately sensed that hunting was for him what fishing was for mom.

As I lie in bed this evening, I think back on my experience with the job interview the day before and realize that stillness only comes when there is a calmness of the mind and body. It is not what happens outside of me, but what happens inside of me that really matter. I remember the scripture that says, "peace be still," and realize that this is the universal message for all who believe in the divine power of Almighty God. I believe this without question. I think my mom and dad understood this also. I roll out of bed and begin to pray. As I do, I become still, waiting patiently, listening in silence for the Holy Spirit to speak to me. My mind and body are rejuvenated with a feeling of love, light, and life. This quiet moment of silence reflects on the stillness in the waters along the Pacific Ocean. I quietly climb back into my bed and sleep until the dawn edges over my window and I begin anew the journey of adventure in a world of new beginnings.

Reality Quotes #3
By Varek Queen

"We all have pockets of intelligence-some are full, some are empty."

"There is a thin line between confidence and arrogance."

"A simple quote softens the day and unlocks bad attitudes."

You Uplift My Spirit
By Linda Garrett

You recognize the light in my soul
Encouraging me with your kindness
Your radiance makes me feel at home
Brightening my day with your smile
Your special warmth overflows onto everyone you meet
I am thankful for the gifts you bring
You uplift my spirit more than I can explain
Your influence on my life means the world to me

Quotes 4
By Lille' McGhee

"A new world unfolds when turning a handicap into clapping hands—I am that voice."

"At age 59, I have played many of roles in life but-now is my time to open the shut curtains and walk out onto CENTER STAGE!"

"Silence can be the greatest source of strength, power, vision, and personal influence…"

Your Radiance Brings Light
By Linda Garrett

A warm ray of light, you are
Shining brightly wherever you go
Sharing a smile, giving a hug
Blessing all souls, along the way
Your divine essence shows clearly
The deep meaning of feeling thankfulness
Spreading love and hope
Throughout your glorious journey
You express gratitude
And remind all of us to do the same
To live for the truth of love
And genuine caring for others
Your radiance brings light
To all who cross your path
What an incredible gift
To feel the full beauty and depth of love
And what a blessing it is to us all
To be touched by your magic
Thank you for revealing the true light that you are

Pregnant With Child
By Lille' McGhee

Today she holds her head HIGH with
grace, dignity and pride
Twenty-eight years ago,
last Tuesday,
she was
pregnant with a boy child.

Once born, she prepared her
son with
life's finest tools;
love, confidence, the best
education, and taught him
life's golden rules.

His life did not follow the career
path that she so carefully
planned.

He carved out a personal path,
discovered girls,
stepped out on faith,
and grew into his own man.

As a young father today,
he embraces the world with
joy and with an open smile.

Lille' McGhee-Queen

He's fully grown up now,
a responsible dad,
with one happy male child.

In the midst of "all" parenting,
lies moments of happiness,
uncertainties and sorrows;
BUT, keep the faith,
And
DO SWEAT THE SMALL STUFF
so pray for a brighter
tomorrow.

Retirement is rapidly approaching
the old lady with child
Her chocolate skin, now velvet,
an "afro", once black, once long,

BUT now,
short, white, and nappy.

She expresses gratitude
and love to the world,
'CAUSE
her son continues
to make her feel happy!

AND, HER GRANDSON
CALLS HER, "DEAR."

NUZHAT!
By Dr. Shehrezard F. Czar

The plane had started to descend into the skies of San Francisco. It had been a long wait for the family. She was returning after more than two years, and the excitement had started to build as each minute passed by...

Nuzhat had been a woman of great taste and flawless liking for houses, flowers, perfumes and travel. With a loving husband by her side, she had ruled a kingdom where everything happened to her likeness and tastes. I love her for one distinctive reason more than any other-she is my mother.

With a good sense of humor, she was naughty, as I recall her from my yester years. It's strange to describe a woman as being naughty, but this word expresses her the best (or maybe humorous). At 5' 4", and a slender body, she was a combination of wit and intelligence, defying her age by many years, something my friends loved most about her. They always thought she was cool.

This reminds me of an incident when I was at medical school. I was standing with a few class fellows, and two seniors. A sparkling, chauffer driven, golden 500 SEL Mercedes Benz drove inside the compound. My seniors (currently, one of the top psychiatrists in Seattle, and the other a leading cardiologist in Aspen, Texas) spun their head 360° in the direction of the car, not taking their eyes off that girl for a moment. "Wow, What a girl!" sighed one. I jumped into the conversation, daring them that I can ask the girl out for dinner within five minutes. The bet was set for a dinner at Sheraton for all those standing with us. I walked towards the car, knocked on the car window, and as it pulled down, I put my face inside the car and said, "Ma'...please come out of the car slowly, and act as you are ready to rock and roll with me." I explained the whole situation to her in one breath, panting. She remained seated inside the car for like ten minutes, and came out with me opening the door for her, and walking in the opposite direction, with my back towards the "losers." What fun we had after my class fellows, who knew her personally, told those seniors, "She's his mother." Fourteen years later at a reunion in Bakersfield, I narrated the incident to their wives, in fact to the whole crowd. As much as the crowd was amused, the two doctors (and it brings laughter as I write it) blushed from pink to red to purple.

She was resistant to worries and depression. The first time I ever saw her cry was when my father died. She went into a shock, and was totally numbed. It took a lot of effort on our part to bring her back to her senses on that fateful day in June 1988. "You know what? You have to be brave and courageous to cry...so cry your heart out," she said to me when my grandfather passed away, two years later. I had looked straight into her eyes with complete disbelief. All through this time, I had thought that her tears were making her weaker, and my father's death would take its toll upon her. And, there she was, giving me a short course in bravery. "Ma, but I thought crying would weaken a person?" "No. It doesn't," she had replied abruptly. "You must mourn his death today. You have lost quite a bit-a grandfather, a mentor, and your very best friend. I cannot afford to see you shatter for the rest of your life." As I broke down, she hugged me tightly against her chest. "Good boy...you have grown today." It took me 14 years to understand what she had meant as she asked me to cry my heart out.

All eyes were set on the arrival gate. We caught her glimpse. She was still waiting for her luggage. She had always been a happy go lucky person. Husband. Kids. Maids. Homes in four cities. Money. But, I never saw her buying jewelry. Instead, it would always be perfumes and crystal. Yes! My house looked more like a store of these two at times. I used to sneak into her bedroom, grab a perfume or two, wrap them beautifully, and pass them over to my girlfriends as presents and gifts. I thus enjoyed the status of being a 'superman' of great taste in perfumes all through my life. Later, as I graduated from the med school, she gave me a bill, giggling, "I want them all back, doctor". I had to pay her through my nose, despite the protests and the innocent faces that I made to avoid paying on behalf of those long gone girlfriends. She had been smarter than I thought. With unmatched patience and a streak of intelligent stubbornness in her, it amazes me sometimes on the time she took to claim back the perfumes. These two elements of her personality, I have inherited, and these mark me as being most persistent and patience.

Med school life was full of fun. I had a group of 20 friends. They all called her Mummy, and adored her as much. She knew what each of them liked to eat, and if we would all gather to spend a weekend at my house, each one of them would be as important as any head of state. When in 1983 she was diagnosed with breast cancer, all 20 of them waited outside surgery, and none went home until she had regained total consciousness, and could tell them their names. Daddy's death, although ultimately was going to be the downfall of her empire, just proved her to be as tall as Mount Everest, and as hard as a diamond in ensuring the longevity of his business. Us!

This is a flash back from the not so distant past, reminiscent of security and happiness we all grew up with as kids. What follows is an account of her battle against cancer, this time it would be uterine cancer, and her attitude makes me a proud man, honored to be her son.

As she came out of the arrival lounge, we rushed towards her, hugging, kissing, and embracing her. "I have just started vaginal bleeding", she whispered in my ears. "Don't tell anybody, but I thought I should let you know doctor." (She would sometimes call me doctor with love.)

It was a jolt. I was horrified and the most scared person on earth at that moment. Despite my long-standing claims of being fearless, the news struck me like I was being possessed by a poltergeist.

As a doctor, I would place cancer on top of my list of differential diagnosis in a postmenopausal, 65-year-old woman. But this was Nuzhat, and she was my mom. And I was devastated. Although, my sister had spotted the sudden change in the hue of my skin, she couldn't understand what had happened. My misery and melancholy could be read as simply as alphabets in black against a white sheet. I got ready for the worse, another characteristic that I had inherited from her.

I called a friend, in Visalia from the car. Mom was trailing in my sister's car. Before she arrived, all 20 of my best friends, the usual gang, had called me on my cell from every corner in the country. It was like a conference call meeting, and we had arrived at certain decisions before I even got home.

The next few days were hectic. She was admitted to a hospital. A preliminary exam revealed bleeding, and after her second appointment, she was called in for dilatation and curettage. A series of tests and exams had to be performed, including biopsy for a definitive diagnosis. The uterine specimen from D&C revealed no pathological evidence of any cancerous growth, and I took a sigh of relief. The CT scan was also normal. NAD: Nothing Abnormal Detected.

From the time that she was admitted for her first examination through the following two months, she bled constantly with varying frequencies and intervals. At one time, I called 911, and rushed her to the hospital because of profuse bleeding. I had never seen so much blood in my 14 years as a doctor than I had seen over the last 2 months…clots, and blood, filling the water closet. I am being haunted by the thought of it, even as I write.

Every Woman Has a Short Story, Men Too!

Her doctor decided to perform a hysterectomy, and a date was set. A day before her hysterectomy, I took her for her pre-op advice. We must have left at around 10 A.M. in the morning. It was a stretched session as her labs had to be done. We returned at around 5 P.M. and then the Armageddon started. She bled like water gushing from a hosepipe. Pads wouldn't work. She would soak them within 5 minutes. I gave her my clean T-Shirt to put along under her pads, and rushed back to the hospital. Half way through, I called 911 from my cell. The paramedics arrived within minutes on Highway 880, which was traffic jammed. I was watching her die slowly right in front of me. Her bleeding would kill her. "Mom"...I looked at a pale structure lying by the driver's seat..."Can you hear me?" "Can you hear me?" I went on and on. "Can you stop yelling for a change? There is no fun dying on a highway bleeding through the uterus," she replied calmly. "I deserve better than that. Will you stop worrying doctor?" By the time paramedics arrived, she had bled almost to the last drop. In the frenzy of the ambulance sirens, I felt my eyes getting wet numerously as I trailed behind it, full throttle.

Upon arrival at the hospital, within minutes, in the very heart of the emergency room, and before they could maintain a lifeline support, she came face-to-face with death. There was no more blood in her veins left to pump through the heart. She had gradually started to fade away from life, going into hypo-volumic shock, just a few hours before her surgery. As she was conscious, the nurse asked her to change into the hospital attire. She asked me to stand outside the rest room, in case she needed me. I removed the blood drenched T-shirt, dripping it all over the floor. The distance from the rest room to her bed was less than 6 feet, and she fell into my arms while struggling to walk that distance. "I want you to take care of the whole family in case I don't walk out alive." I gathered my energies to smile, desperately trying to remain composed. "No! I won't Ma. It's your family. You better be there for them if they need you." As I said this, she had lost consciousness.

Between her operation, scheduled for the next day in the morning, to the life saving efforts in the emergency, they had transfused blood, and maintained her vitals for the night. I saw her turning from dull pale to normal pink, and I felt like I was being born again. She had won the worst battle of her life. She was ready for the second fight.

Dr. Pierce had been her doctor from day one. She was very concerned with the incidences of the previous night. The team having decided that she was stable for surgery, she smiled at me and said, "This is much safer than what she went through last night." I knew she was in safe hands, and I wished I had some questions of concern. "Ugh! Sometimes, it's no fun to be a doctor." As I said this to myself, I realized it was the Nuzhat inside me, with her full sense of humor, not sparing any moment in life to smile about.

Her surgery was perfect, meticulous modern wonder of science. Dr. Pierce apprised me of her findings. She knew my concerns. "No cancerous growth on visual examination. I have thoroughly examined all the adjoining areas, reaching far into the abdominal cavity. I have sent the flushed water for microscopic pathology, as well as samples from the nodes." Her post-op recovery was speedy. Things looked good.

This current surgery takes me back to 1983 when she was operated on for breast cancer. Losing a body part to the "bio-hazard bin" cannot be easy for any one in the world. But she took it so lightly. "Radiation is even simpler. Who says no pain, no gain? It doesn't hurt, and you walk out fine."

Dr. Ahmad, her surgeon and also one of our professors at the med school back in '83, was not a man who would smile at all. Though he was an absolutely composed man with perfect calm, we as students dreaded him for not ever smiling. I saw him laugh with my mother. I think her innocence was more amusing to him than her sense of humor. I made some good money betting with my friends on a 'smiling and laughing Dr. Ahmad'.

I received a call from Dr. Pierce after a few days. Nodal metastasis was positive. The tumor board at the hospital referred her to a comprehensive cancer center where Dr. Swift ran her through a preparatory phase for radiotherapy. The radiotherapy was going to be a time consuming event, spreading over weeks. Upon my request, her case was shifted to the Radio Oncology Center. Dr. Su, upon physical examination, referred her to the Medical Center. A growth was found on the vaginal cavity, and they didn't want to risk an extensive area, stretching to mid-thoracic cavity, being exposed to extensive radiotherapy.

Dr. Chan is a man with deep eyes but definitely a smiling face. He took over from that point on. The stage of her cancer was diagnosed at C3, which is very advanced. What a silent invasion Nuzhat had undergone. We opted for invasive chemotherapy. She had a distinctively palpable supra-clavicular node, which was set as a reference point to gauge the effect of treatment.

The first two treatments took a heavy toll on Mummy. I don't want to go into those details, but suffice it to say, she had to return to the hospital within three days after each chemo due to severe dehydration, nausea and vomiting. Dr. Chan decided to lower the dose and expand it to 6 treatments as opposed to four, spreading over an interval of three weeks between each dose. As we returned, and the doctor was examining her, I said, "Dr. Chan, I think I might have lost my touch, for there was no nodule palpable any more in the supra-clavicular area". "I am glad I have lost my touch too," he smiled back with shining eyes. "Chemo has worked wonderfully, and I think we should continue with the same drugs, even though I was considering other options." We both agreed to continue with the same medicines.

Mummy is now in the final phase of her chemo. With four treatments in place, and due to the dosage lowered by 20 percent, she would soon be ready for the 5th round. As I was writing about her, I decided to finish her story by interviewing her on the events, which had affected her life over the last one year.

Here is a summary of what she had to say about everything in response to my different questions:
"I felt nothing as I found out that I had cancer. I had it before; I ran the risk of remission. I got it again. I am a human in all sense. I never feared it. Period. I wasn't sacred of the bleeding which had started to grow extensive, but blood loss has its own complications. I felt weak, breathless, and my legs would tremble with weakness. Like one time, I was taking a shower, and blood started to gush out. I could feel the clots slipping down on my legs, and water turning red. You had asked me to keep the door open just in case that I might need help. But I continued with the shower. I thought now that I am bleeding, I should finish my shower. About the night at the emergency that you are referring to, I was ready to die. No. I wasn't sacred. It would be foolish to be scared of something, which is inevitable, and death is inevitable. I had given cancer just about its due chance…it had lived on my flesh without telling me, and had trespassed. I am going to kick it out of my system now that I know it came uninvited. It did try to make me bleed to death, but I have survived. Now, it has to go. I would die of anything but cancer. And to this I stand committed. Have I considered it a hilarious situation? Yes! Certainly. I think I nurtured this thief for too long, and it took me for granted.

You want me to sum it all. Well! Having a good sense of humor makes life very easy. It changes the way you look at things, from a different angle, and a different perspective. Wit has to be handled with great subtleness. You maintain an intricate balance between what is and what's not. Women want men who can make them laugh. Pick up a magazine, and humor is at the top of the list of every woman's ideal partner. They forget that men also need women who can make them laugh. We are here for a short period of time. We should cherish each moment to its fullest. Laugh, smile, chuckle or giggle, but make sure you exercise your facial muscles in the right direction. And before you send this story out about me, don't you dare think that I was born in a small town circus ring. Life is one big happy circus! I wish I could put that on my passport…Place of Birth: "Circus".

Quotes 5
By Lille' McGhee

"There is a PLUS in every MINUS-assess the situation and then do the MATH."

"Let the sunlight come into your garden and spirit into your heart."

"Wealth, without greed, clearly describes a millionaire's true character."

Reality Quotes #4
By Varek Queen

"There is nothing more frightening than IGNORANCE in ACTION!"

"Picky and lonely are best friends."

"Life is about switching roles - once parents, now child!"

The Female Sprinter

By Lille' McGhee

It's Monday morning,
at the crack of dawn,
she begins another day;

Milking the cows,
feeding the chicken,
fresh eggs in the hay.

Inside the house, she yells,
"Wake up, you kids,
come down those steps,
say your prayers, and then
eat your food."

"Get dressed,
comb your hair,
go catch the
bus for school."

"Listen to the teachers,
do your very best,
make good grades,
and follow the
Principal's Rules,

'CAUSE, I don't want

a letter from the teacher
today, saying that you acted like
a clown at school."

Most of mom's life,
like dad's,
was spent raising
a spiritual family
on the Carolina's country
farms.

Sprinting through the
green pastures, tobacco fields,
AND
working long hours
in the hot sun.

They insisted that each
child gets, at minimum,
a high school education.
With a diploma or
college degree,
in hand, they could
get into a good
occupation.

Dad died, July 1986,
with cancer of the throat;

Mom was alone,
without her man,
for the very first time,
AND
her emotions were

getting very low.

One night an Angel,
at her bedside
whispered, "You will never be
left alone, 'CAUSE,
the man you married,
loves you still.
He's waiting at
Heaven's Throne!"

Feels Like Home

By Linda Garrett

Having you for a friend feels like home
A place where I can be totally honest with you and myself
Expressing how I feel with no fear of being judged
I feel so comfortable with you
I know you will be my friend forever
No matter what I say or how I behave
As if nothing in this world could separate us
I feel so safe with you
With your friendship I always feel supported
You have created a meaningful place in my life
A place where I can follow my dreams
I can make mistakes and be forgiven
There is nothing we cannot talk about
We are blessed with the gift of divine love
That, my friend, is a sacred place
Where two people can feel secure and at ease
In the warmth of love, with no conditions
A place, where I feel at home, with you

The Day I Saw the Angels
By Carolyn Jolly Douglas

Every person has a story to tell. Let me tell you about the day I saw the angels.

Oh, did I get your attention? I hope so because if you have ever wondered about whether or not angels are present with us, then I want to offer my story for you to contemplate. You can then draw your own conclusion.

Several years ago, I began my pursuit of the spiritual life. What I mean by this is that I really wanted to understand the Spirit and my relationship to God. I was raised in a Christian household, attended church religiously twice on Sundays, and at least once during the week for choir rehearsal. I learned to read the Bible and to explain the scriptures. After becoming an adult, I had more of a say in whether to go or not to go to church, and where I should go.

Since I had learned very early that I had a spiritual life, I was interested in finding the right place for myself to explore. Many thoughts ran through my mind about how people in other spiritual traditions connected with God. So I allowed myself to read and study other religions. This turned out to be an awesome experience in the study of God and I availed myself to perform some of the spiritual practices that called to me. This opened my heart to sensing a more expansive awareness of the Spirit.

One day I got the idea in my head to sing to God. I began to sing traditional hymns that I had learned in Sunday school, and then moved on to popular songs that I heard on the religious radio station. Later I pared down my program or repertoire to those songs that were my favorites of all times. Every evening after dinner, but before going to bed, I sang to God. This practice went on for a long time.

As I sang, I began to imagine that I was singing with the choir of angels that I was taught about in Sunday school. These angels "lived in heaven" with God and were dispensed by God to assist humans in their lives. I felt honored to be in that choir and soon allowed myself to sing with complete abandonment. You see, I had also been taught that angels sang so beautifully that my voice could blend in with theirs and not stand out. When we sang together, there wasn't a note that I could not sing or a melody that I could not carry. I often felt myself moved into a state of euphoria, in ecstasy. And, in this state of being is when I felt that God was very close to me.

One Sunday morning, the music for the worship service was extremely moving. With the opening of the service, the entire congregation sang as one voice with all heart and soul. Then following the program guide, the classical pianist began playing the Lord's Prayer. A soloist stepped forward in the pulpit to sing, and we knew to just listen. I closed my eyes to eliminate any distractions and to absorb the musical talents of these individuals. Her voice was perfect and pure, hitting every note with the right precision and expressing each word with distinguishable clarity. Together they were creating the perfect expression of worship and praise. Whether through skill or being caught up in the doing, the produced sound was angelic. I was captivated in the sacred moment and whisked away from the present to some place ethereal.

As the song neared its ending, I felt a pang of regret. I wanted it to last because I was experiencing that wonderful euphoria. And it was a good place to be because I felt God in this ecstasy. With the last sounds of the music, I began to open my eyes. To my delight, I saw an angel dressed in white kneeling before me with its hands clasped in prayer over my hands. I sensed that we both had been singing to God. As the soloist ended the song, the angel moved away from me to the pulpit area hovering for a second or two then moved to the back of the room where it joined two other angels. I blinked my eyes and they were gone. A sense of surprise and awe flushed over me. Did I just see what I thought I saw? I looked around to see if anyone else had seen the same thing, but saw no indication of it.

It was now time to move on to the next thing in the service. The minister began to speak.

Later as I contemplated this numinous experience, I again felt that same sense of awe as I interpreted for myself what I thought this vision meant. Angels, the messengers of God, observe the activities of humans. It meant the Divine is always near, always close by, and always right where I am. What a thought! What a comforting thought!

Sometimes we need to have an experience or a moment of clarity to remind us that the presence of the Spirit or God is always with us.

Whether I saw angels with my physical eyes, or through an inner vision or awareness is not the relevant issue to me. What is important to me is how I have used that experience to support my faith during challenging times. The memory of it has served me well over the years, during moments of uncertainty and doubt. It is comforting to know that the presence of the Spirit is always with me. And, I still sing to God.

Quotes 6
By Lille' McGhee

"Search for the truth even when the evidence reflects otherwise…"

"Don't slow down when you become successful-slow down at the right time!"

"To reach the maximum level of success, raise the bar."

An Unfinished Masterpiece: High School Years (1985-1987)

By Varek Queen

Over the past two years, I have developed from a young boy into a young man. I have undergone changes intellectually, emotionally, physically, and socially. My perspectives have gone from general to focus.

Intellectually, my interests and abilities have varied widely through the different stages of development. My academic performance has deteriorated steadily for the past three years. I have allowed too many distractions to affect my interest level, my ability to concentrate, and my overall performance. I have allowed personal interests, relationships, and problems to interfere with my studies.

My ability to deal with and correct problems is vastly better than it was six months ago. Problem recognition is the first step to problem resolution. My problems are that I am too easily distracted and allow personal problems to affect my attitude and interest levels. I am learning to channel the enormous amounts of pressure placed upon me to achieve academic excellence. I know my grades have not been very good (and still aren't), but they are improving overall and my determination to see them increase will certainly pay off in the long run. I am now at the stage where my performance is improving overall, but I still suffer occasional setbacks, or find myself trapped with too much to do and too little time to do it. Tonight, for example, I have two exams to study for, a paper to finish that was half done, and the usual amount of homework to complete.

Every Woman Has a Short Story, Men Too!

I still need to work on managing my time better, improving my memory skills, and learning not to freeze-up in the middle of a test. The biggest tool I have to work with is an improving self-image and self-confidence. I know that I can do better, and I am determined that I will.

Emotionally, I have changed a lot over the last two years. My ability to recognize and express feelings has grown tremendously. I have learned to control my anger and release it in various ways. When I was younger, I turned to violence and hostility as a way to express myself. I would let these emotions build up inside of me and at a given time and place would release them on either something or somebody. Punching your hand through a wall only hurts your hand, puts a hole in the wall, and gets you in more trouble, which makes you more frustrated, and angrier, and on and on it goes.

I feel as though I have grown out of this childish mode of expression. I now know how to talk things out, as well as think things through. I'm not saying that the feelings of violence or hostility don't exist; I simply have learned how to better deal with them. I now channel my physical aggression into running laps or pumping iron.

Physically, I have gone through many changes. I have developed from a little kid into a big kid. Between the ages of 14 and 16, my weight has varied from 135 to 160 pounds and my height increased from 5'6" to 5'10". Curiously, my shoe size has gone from a size 12 to a 10 ½. I don't really care, and my father is real happy, because now he can wear my basketball shoes.

My body structure has changed from boyish to manly. My skinny legs grew hairy and muscular. My bird chest expanded and developed. My hair changed from curly to wavy, and has changed colors from brown to black. The peach-fuzz on my upper lip grew into a mustache and I now have a passable beard. My eyebrows have thickened. I am especially glad that my voice went from high to low. The only thing that has remained the same is my size 29 waist. I am much more stronger, and my body is starting to show hard lines of muscle separation and development.

Socially, I have changed in several ways. I have always had male and female friends, but the boys had always outnumbered the girls. Now, it's the opposite. I find it more enjoyable to talk to and be with girls than boys. The other big change is that instead of wanting to do things and go places, I now have the ability to do so-I have a car. Now, if I only had some money to do all those things.

One month before I was sixteen, I received a navy blue Buick Skylark as a Christmas present. A few months later, I also had access to a gray and a black one, as well. The black one was fantastic-brand new, all digital dash, and a turbo-charged engine. My father let me drive it for two months during the summer until he hired a new sales rep and assigned the car to him. My car was okay, but it was always in the shop for repairs and it looked like some thing a little old lady would drive, and handled like a baby tank.

This August, I got a new car. This really changed my social life. My new Renault Encore Sport hatchback was a new experience. The 1.7 liter fuel-injected engine felt a lot better than the V-6 in my Skylark. The car is smaller, sportier, and handles much better, and I don't feel like a 40-year old businessman with a wife and three kids. When everybody saw me driving around in my new little sports car, they all wanted to go everywhere with me. I even got to charge them for gas.

Writing about cars is a rather superficial way to end a paper about my physical, emotional, and intellectual development. But, as I said earlier, my time management still needs a lot of work, and I do have two tests to study for, and phone calls to return (if you ignore the girls too much they'll learn to ignore you), and it's midnight and I'm tired. Goodnight.

Reality Quotes #5
By Varek Queen

"Nothing ever changes without FIRST acknowledging the need for change."

"True happiness does not come from having something-it comes from being a part of something within."

"Born to Succeed," She Says...
By Lille′ McGhee

It's 5 minutes before the
day breaks;
Darkness has not yet
touched daylight.

Her mind is filled with
creative thoughts;
She's almost ready to
write.

A choice was hers to
stay in bed,
and sneak in that
one extra hour,
BUT instead she jumps
up with vigor,
fetches a cup of tea,
and writes with
female power!

She avoids long
discussions,
also pointless political
debates.

She taps into her talents

Every Woman Has a Short Story, Men Too!

That God continues
to create.
Try waking up today
with passion, impact
and vision,
Then listen to what the spirit
Is trying to say.
'Cause there is a genius inside
of you,
Let it come out in
its own way.

Her day is almost over;
night is falling upon
the winter leaves.

Remember this one thing,
if nothing else,
"Every Child is Born to Succeed."

My Teacher
By Linda Garrett

You are teaching me…
how to love without fear
to be myself, whatever form that may take
to express my feelings and emotions
that love doesn't have to feel scary or intimidating
to accept myself and others exactly as they are
where a positive attitude can help others and yourself
the importance of treating others as you wish to be treated
that which is inside someone's soul is what really matters
how loving and giving bring meaning to life
to tell the truth and be open is one of the most valuable gifts two people can share
what it feels like to be respected, treasured, and cherished
to hear my inner voice clearly and to trust it
that it is my soul that feels so comfortable at home in your heart
to follow divine guidance as it leads me to you

Leaving My Mother's Nest

By Angela Stephine Woods

In March 1980, I arose to a cold brisk Greensboro, North Carolina morning. My life was about to go into a major tailspin. I was about to embark on the most important aspect of my life. Leaving my mother's nest-what a scary thought.

I had attended junior college, but decided that it wasn't what I wanted-I needed something totally different, and I made a drastic decision. My mind was racing with thoughts of "can I do this" or "would my journey be a failure". Although the thought of failure was there, my determination overcame it.

The smell of breakfast cooking consumed the house and I knew that my mother was in the kitchen doing what she had done for as long as I could remember. She wasn't too thrilled about the decision that I had made, but she supported me.

After finishing breakfast, my mother and I sat down to talk about my new journey. My bags were already packed and I had my bus ticket to my next destination. It's ten o'clock now and my other family member's have arrived to say "good luck". My heart was filled with love for everyone and having to leave was hard for me, but I knew that I needed a change in my life. Not being able to see my grandparents on a daily basis would be very difficult. Both of them were such a source of strength for me and we were very close. My grandmother's birthday was on the 12th of March, so we had our time together before her birthday. (I never spent another birthday with my grandmother. She died suddenly on August 13, 1990). It's now time to leave for the bus station. As I looked at everyone, I could see their sadness of my leaving, but also the joy of what I was about to do. We all got into our cars and headed for the bus station.

At the station, I checked my suitcase in and I waited with my family for the bus to arrive. As my bus arrived, I kissed each and every family member. I picked up my carry-on bag and as I walked toward the exit, they all called out, "Angela," and I turned around. As I turned around, they were all holding up a huge sign: GO NAVY.

After arriving in Charlotte, North Carolina, I and other recruits were separated into groups. We were given keys to our hotel rooms. It's still March 11th, and this was our last night of freedom as civilians, because tomorrow we were going to take the most important step of our lives.

It's the morning of March 12th, and we are all eating breakfast waiting for the bus to take us to the Induction Center in Charlotte. The thought crossed my mind that now was the time to back out before taking the oath. Once you have taken that oath, there was no turning back. After signing a lot of papers, it is time to take the oath. I looked around the room and no one was leaving. My legs are jelly now and my heart is beating fast, but I knew that I wanted to do this.

The time is now, and we are all about to take the oath, while standing in front of the United States flag. Our right hand rose pledging to "Support and Defend the Constitution of the United States". Oh, what a powerful pledge that was for me, and still is to this day. Wow, I was now a member of the United States Navy.

After taking the pledge, we all went back to the hotel to have dinner and wait to be taken to the airport on our next journey.

We departed from Charlotte International Airport around 7:30 P.M. and arrived at the Recruit Training Command in Orlando, Florida around 10:00 P.M., on March 12, 1980, for boot camp.

We are all very tired. We were then taken to a large room with lots of beds. We each choose a bed and were told to get some sleep. My adrenalin was so pumped up that I couldn't sleep. When I finally got tired, I laid my head down around 1:00 A.M. At 3:00 A.M., we were all awaken to a large sound of a trashcan being thrown down the isle and this individual yelling, "Get up now!" What a way to be awakened but we had no choice; there was no time to sleep. What a shock!

We were all marched (horribly), with our Drill Sergeants yelling, to breakfast with only twenty minutes to eat and get back in formation. The sun is now up and we went to get fitted for our uniforms. After getting fitted we went back to our permanent barracks. Our company was called KO67.

Each week we went to classes to study Naval history. We also learned how to fold our clothes in a military style, clean, make beds, physical education and how to swim. I never liked swimming, so I had to overcome that fault. I had to go to extra swim classes just to learn how to float. I am afraid of heights and each time I went, I froze but I finally got up the nerve to step off a 12-foot diving board. Oh, what a joy that was for me. I felt such an accomplishment on my new journey.

After so much to learn and do it's now time for graduation. It's May 15, 1980. I am so excited. I have lived with these women for 12 weeks and we have bonded; now after graduation, we will all be going in different military career paths. It's sad to leave these ladies, but we are all filled with so much joy and happiness.

There was one disappointment on my graduation day-since my mom doesn't fly, none of my family members attended. Although it did matter, I marched that parade field in front of that crowd with such a joy in my heart.

After graduation, we all left on different adventures. I was sent to Meridian, MS for seven weeks of school. Oh, what a culture shock Meridian was. Being there was my first time exposed to racism. I could not believe that blacks had one side of the street to walk on and whites the other. The military base was really the only safe place to be, so you took your chances when you went into the town of Meridian. I hated Meridian and having that feeling gave me the drive to get out of that town as quickly as possible, and I did it in five weeks.

When I graduated from school in Mississippi and received my diploma, I was sent to Key West, FL, which was a most joyous adventure for me. I lived in Key West for four years and would love to return someday.

The city of Key West and its citizens taught me so much about how to deal with all different types of people, and I carry that with me now.

While in Key West, my Commanding Officer sent me to the Naval Justice School in Newport, RI so that I could become a paralegal to military lawyers.

I was hand picked to attend this school. The job was very intense and confidentiality was essential, and I loved my job. I worked in that job for two years. In January 1984, my Commanding Officer put me in for Special Assignment to the American Embassy, which was located in London, England. I got the assignment, but I didn't accept it. I chose to go on a military ship in Charleston, SC. As I look back on my decision, I know that I made a mistake. I was independent, but in my soul I was still my mama's oldest daughter and she still had a hold on me.

Arriving in Charleston, was a real culture shock for me. After arriving, I, along with others, were taken on a tour of the city and we went to a park called the "Battery", which was on the water where you could look and see Fort Sumter. We also went to the business district to get the history of Charleston, and to my disbelief was a true hanging block where slaves had been hung. After seeing that, I was scared and totally disgusted. Charleston is such a beautiful and cultural city, but some things need to be demolished.

I didn't live in Charleston though; I lived in a small town called Goose Creek, where my ship was moored. I went to work everyday and I enjoyed myself. I worked for the Captain of the

Every Woman Has a Short Story, Men Too!

ship and I had my own office. There were 1200 people on my ship and 600 of them were females. Wow, what a ratio. I met a fellow sailor on the ship and we began dating in August of 1984. In November 1984, I became pregnant. I had just turned 25 and I was about to become a mother.

It was time for me to leave the ship. I hated to leave, but Navy regulations prohibit "pregnant females" to be on military ships. As I walk down the plank, I refuse to look back. My heart is aching because I wanted to stay, but I know in my heart that I can't. I am now on my way to North Carolina to see my family. Afterwards, I will leave for Virginia. My mom is still in denial that I am with child and I know that she doesn't approve. That is her problem and not my problem. I am an adult now but in my heart I still need her approval. Lord, why can't I please my mom? I need her approval so much and I don't know why. My childhood was normal according to "SOCIETY", but I grew up with a single mom (widowed) who raised three kids. My mom worked hard to support all of us, and her strength is what I have believed in all of my life. I love my mom-she did an excellent job and raised us well.

My oldest son was born on August 16, 1985, which happened to be on my birthday and what a joy that was for me. We resided in Virginia until January 1987 at which time I received military orders to move to Jacksonville, Florida. My new job was with a command that went overseas for six months at a time.

It's August of 1988 and I am in glorious Bermuda. I miss my son so much. He is in North Carolina. The separation is difficult, but I managed by working hard, which kept my mind busy. An opportunity has come up for me to visit the most exciting place in the world, that I can think. I am now about to go to Rio De Janeiro, Brazil for two weeks with the military. I am so excited that I can't stand it.

November 1988, I, along with others from my command, arrive in Brazil. I can't believe it. The country is so populated, poor and rich. I see children on the street trying to sell items to the tourist, and also in the hotel sections of the city. You have to be able to know how to speak Portugease in order to understand how much something cost. We drove by the poor side of town and the "tourist" part of town. Oh, what a difference. I'm living in a high-rise hotel called the Meridian right on the strip with the beach across the street. The food is cheap and so are the other commodities. I loved the country and I will never forget my visit there.

Back in Bermuda and we have one month left here. The shopping, beaches, and going to the town of Hamilton to see the cruise ships come in was great. I didn't want to leave Bermuda, but it's time to get back to my son.

I'm back in Jacksonville, Florida and I am about to go and get my son from North Carolina. I've moved into my new apartment to get ready for my son. I enrolled him in school. He is now in Kindergarten. It's so hard, sometimes, being a single parent, but I managed. It's now time for me to tell him that I have to go away and take him back to my mother in North Carolina.

It's January 1990 and I am about to go and spend six months in Sigonela, Sicily. My son is in North Carolina with my family right now. I moved out of the apartment and put my furniture in storage until I return. Sigonella is a beautiful country. The shopping is great and the people are wonderful. I'm working twelve hours a day now. My job was very confidential.

On May 10, 1990 I received a call from the Red Cross telling me that my brother had died. I went home immediately. I flew for a total of 30 hours (with time change), but it seemed as if I had flown forever. I arrived home at 2:30 A.M. Friday morning, May 11, 1990.

At home it's my job to write his obituary and take his suit to the cleaners. As usual, everyone comes over bringing food and offering their sympathy. I saw many people that didn't even know my brother, but they knew my mom. My brother was buried at our family church next to my grandfather.

It's time to return to Sicily. I only have a few weeks left before I return to Florida.

I'm back in Florida and it's June. The weather is hot but it feels good to be back. I'm on my way to get my son and bring him back to Florida with me.

It's back to work for me, and school for my son. Once a week, I always called my grandmother. On August 13, 1990, I called her and she didn't answer. That wasn't like her. I then called my mom and she wasn't home either, so I called my grandmother's sister. She told me that my grandmother was in the hospital. I'm in a panic mode now and my heart is beating rapidly. I finally got in contact with my mom and asked her how my grandmother was. I heard this silence in her voice, and then the words that my grandmother had died. After hearing those words, I dropped the phone and I started to scream so loud that I couldn't stop. I returned home once again to bury another family member. My grandmother and brother died three months and four days apart. The year of 1990 wasn't a good year for me. No matter how I felt, I had to return to my military duty and move on.

In July 1991, I received new orders to leave Florida and move to Norfolk, Virginia.

I reported to my new command and I moved into my new office. I was appointed the Office Supervisor and I have five other people working for me. I like my new job. I enjoyed the fact that I didn't have to leave my son again.

Life was good and I was happy. I had a fiancé and we were about to become parents. On April 23, 1992, I gave birth to a daughter. In December 1993, I was chosen as Sailor of the Year for my command. That was such a great honor. On March 6, 1994, I gave birth to a son. My time is getting shorter at my command now. I am due to either get out of the Navy or re-enlist.

It's 1995 and the military is downsizing and if a sailor has fifteen years or more and wanted to retire, then they could with full benefits. Even though I had planned on doing twenty years in the military, I knew that it was my time to leave. I was pleased with the success in rank that I had achieved. I entered the Navy as a Seaman Recruit (E-1) and I will be retiring as a First Class Petty Officer. It's October 31, 1995 and I am retiring from the Navy with sixteen and a half years of Honorable Service. My heart was filled with sadness but also with much joy. My children and I were about to start a new life together.

Divine Fortune
By Linda Garrett

You have been so understanding
Through all my ups and downs
Endlessly supporting me along my path
I would not be where I am now, without you
As I move forward, toward my true essence
You are a vital part of my expansion
Nurturing my growth with your gentle kindness
And touching my heart with your magic and grace
My soul overflows with gratitude
For the sacredness of your love
I have found a divine fortune in you
A vision of heavenly light
Your ability to give, and keep giving
Is such a precious treasure
I am so thankful for every day
That I am blessed by your presence in my life

God's Everywhere
By Lille' McGhee

No matter where I go,
God always beats
Me there.

Whether it's on
Dry land,
At sea,
Or flying
In mid-air.

With God as
A security;
I am in very
Good hands.

I can now climb
Life's HIGHEST
Mountains,
Without a
Written business
Plan.

Each day I wake
Up, with gratitude
And
A deep sense of pride.

Every Woman Has a Short Story, Men Too!

At last I can
See the
Promised Land,
'Cause God is right
Here by my side…GOD IS EVERYWHERE

Reality Quotes #6

By Varek Queen

"Wisdom is beyond prize, so be grateful if you have wisdom."

"It is false bravery if there is no F-E-A-R involved."

"Life is a random series of events that occur before birth, during birth, and after birth."

Hold on to the Vision

By Linda Garrett

Miracles happen when you truly believe they are possible
Your inner voice will guide you, if you are steadfast in knowing
The voice speaks the truth, with divine power and wisdom
Trust in yourself, for all other things in life can come and go
Hold on to the Vision without letting go
And know in your heart that amazing things happen
With love, trust and faith in yourself
and in the incredible powers of the universe
the truth of your visions will become clear
and you will find peace, love and harmony
In the connection with your own divine spirit

How to Support a Hurting Spouse
By Joyce Sherman

We met at the altar all starry eyed and eager to recite the marriage vows before friends, family members and God. "I will honor, cherish, and love through sickness and health, until death do we part." We gave a warm embrace to each other and walked the aisle with smiles and love in our hearts for each other, with the expectation of many happy years of marriage together.

I had married a man of tall stature, smart, handsome and most of all a Christian. I was very happy to become his wife.

As the years passed, we shared many wonderful life experiences together, and we were excited about future plans.

We have three children: Al, Morris and Katherine, and God has truly blessed us with four beautiful grandchildren: Lovell, Shaffon, Maya and Levi. They are all healthy, loving and smart. I thank God for each one of them.

My husband was born with a disease called Keloids. It is a genetic skin disorder. His mother showed visible signs of the skin disorder, on her right shoulder. His father was a carrier of the skin disorder.

Keloids are sometimes called, hypertrophic scars. They are an overgrowth of scar tissue at the site of a skin injury. Keloids will develop with such skin injuries as surgical incisions, traumatic wounds, vaccination sites, burns, chickenpox, acne, or even minor scratches. (MedLine Plus, Health Information, Medical Encyclopedia)

They are common in patients of West African and Asian origin. (O'Sullivan S T O'Connor T P, O'Shaughnessy M. Aetiology and management of hypertrophic scars Ann R Coll Surg 1996: 78: 168-175.)

Keloidosis is a term used when multiple or repeated Keloids are produced. My husband was considered keloidosis.

If you have never seen keloids, they look like overgrown blisters. They consist of hard, raised scar tissue that may be slightly pink or whitish. They itch and are painful, and some keloids grow to be quite large. You might remember, in the earlier years, when individuals had their ears pierced and a bump would develop at the back of their earlobes. That was likely a keloid.

The Keloids on my husband began to grow during 1953 (at age 5), and from 1984 on, the Keloids grew like wildfire on his chest, neck and face. They began to deplete his blood supply, causing him to become very anemic and tired, also in addition to restricting his neck motion, he would sleep most of the day. The sleeping was a way to manage the pain.

Before his last operation, in 2003, the Keloids had grown to measure at least 2 to 3 inches on the neck and face, and would just hang.

He began to seek out doctors for help to have the Keloids removed. We heard of a specialist in the Los Angeles area. We called for an appointment and the doctor was kind enough to see him. We booked a flight and flew to Los Angeles for the medical appointment. After the examination, the doctor explained that he normally performed surgery on much smaller Keloids than those on my husband's neck, face and chest.

He had the first set of Keloids removed from his chest area, but they returned. He had the ones removed from his neck and they returned. They began to grow back after the surgery and cover his ear opening. They affected his ability to chew and later caused TMJ (Temporomandibular).

Before any surgery could be performed, it was necessary for him to have blood transfusions. After each surgery, the doctor recommended radiation treatment. These procedures caused hair loss on his head and eyebrows. The actual procedure was to retard the growth cell of the Keloids.

Each surgery, of which he had six in 2003, the doctor required him to stay in the hospital a minimum of five days to minimize the chance of infection. (His stay was longer than most heart patients.)

Each time he was sent home after surgery, it was necessary for him to have an in-home nurse to take care of the wounds and bandages. This was necessary three times a day, to minimize infection, and went on for several months. Each time he had surgery, the procedures began again.

The in-home nurse instructed me on how to change the bandages. I must admit that I had gotten pretty good with the procedure. I would come home daily on my lunch break and prepare lunch and change the bandages.

My husband decided one day to tell the nurse that I could change the bandage all by myself, and her services were no longer needed. Little did he know that I needed her help in more ways than one. To clean the wound and prepare bandages were chores in itself. Just to see the deep wounds would beef up anyone's prayer life. To change the bandages was nerve racking because they had grafted skin off his thigh as replacement skin for his face. The skin was so thin that, if you were to hold it to the light, you could literally see through it. The nerve-racking part was that the wound and bandage had to be handled with extreme care. I had to be very focused and not distracted in the least way. Otherwise, the care the doctors took and the pain my husband had already endured would have been in vain. If I had taken the bandages off wrong, in any way, the drafted skin would either lift or peel away. I didn't want that to happen.

The Keloids not only looked bad, they gave him a gross appearance. They would bleed on their own and the infection was overwhelming. You could smell his trail. Due to the smell, to ride in a car with him was unbearable. I had a cough that wouldn't go

Every Woman Has a Short Story, Men Too!

away and I believe that it was due to constantly smelling the infection.

My husband suffers, even today, with constant pain, bleeding, and sometimes, mild infection. Even when he sleeps, I hear him cry out in pain.

Doctors across the country say that my husband's Keloid is the worst they've ever seen. My husband has labeled himself as the poster *child* of keloid. He jokingly says, "if you look up Keloid in the dictionary, you would see his face".

People in the street would stare, point and make rude remarks. In a way, I didn't blame them. Most people do not know anything about Keloids. There is not a whole lot known or written about the skin disorder. The word keloid is not found in the Webster dictionary.

A non-Christian once said, "I should pack my bags and leave." They questioned my motives for wanting to continue the marriage.

Friends would say, "Honey, if it was me, when I saw that first bump, I would have packed my bags and ran as fast and hard as I could."

Family members were kind and loving. Thank God for loving families.

Travel was not easy either for him. He is an engineer and his position requires him to do extensive travel both nationally and internationally. I could only imagine the torture he would endure while traveling. The times I have traveled with him, I have noticed that no one wanted to stand near him or associate with him. What they didn't know was the character of the man, my loving husband. They only saw the outer appearance.

I didn't know and I'm sure that my husband didn't know that he would be affected by Keloids for the rest of his life. Sure his mother showed visible signs of Keloids, but they were so minor that no one looked at them seriously.

His father was a carrier of the skin disorder. He has an uncle that is affected, and a niece. No one gave it a good long hard look and considered what he would be facing in his later years, and for the duration of his life.

I would pray daily for his healing and that a doctor somewhere would be able to help him. I hated to see him suffer day after day, and to know that Keloids would be with him for a lifetime.

Early on I knew this situation was too big for me. There was nothing that I could do except pray and keep the faith. I had to realize when things are too big for me; I need to turn them over to Christ.

I did hear my husband on occasion ask God, "Why did this have to happen to me?" "What can I do to quickly resolve this problem?" "How long will it take me to change this situation?" I would have asked the same questions, if I were the one affected with this severe disease.

He later realized that God had allowed this disorder so that He would be glorified (Peter 4: 12-13; John 11:1-4). He also realized that God would make his trial a blessing for him. The last of the six operations I mentioned, God spoke to him and told him to share his story to others as a testimony. He began writing the material to present at seminars, and started several books, all centered on his Keloids and how God was with him all the time.

He leaned on the scripture that God said, "He will never leave you nor forsake you." "When thou are in tribulation, and all these things are come upon thee, even in the latter day, if thou turn to the Lord thy God, and shalt be obedient unto his voice, for the Lord thy God is a merciful God; he will not forsake thee, neither destroy thee, nor forget the covenant of thy fathers which he sware unto thee" (Deut. 4:30, 31).

Jesus does all things well. My spouse revised his earlier statement by instead of asking God how he could get out of the situation, he asked, "How can God be glorified in the situation he faces?"

I have shared some gory details of my husband's Keloids with you. I did it to show that not only has my family been affected by trials and tribulations but your family may also incur some. If trials come upon you or your spouse, it will not be the end of the world. Place your faith in Jesus Christ, who is faithful, he will see you through.

Beware of ungodly advice. A person told me that when they saw the first bump they would have packed their clothes and ran.

I want those of you who read this book to be encouraged in supporting your spouse because we all will deal with trials in our lives, but exercise the hope that Christ has given you. Tomorrow will bring about a change and know it will be exactly as God has planned it to be.

My husband's plight seems pretty bad to me, but I knew that I had to be there by his side to support him and see him through this. I had to have faith that my God was and is with him each and every day.

Everyone has something that they are dealing with, if they are honest. There are certain things you can't hide from in society, family, or God and in my husband's case, Keloids was one of them. The best way to handle life's situations is to establish a strong relationship with God.

Your relationship with God and your attitude about the situation will determine how you will make it from day-to-day.

My husband loves the Lord and also me. He has exercised faith and belief that this life on earth is temporary; that Jesus had gone to prepare a place for him and that one day for him there will be no more pain and sorrow. My husband's hope is in the word of God.

Lille' McGhee-Queen

Life on earth is a test-this is seen throughout the Bible. God continually tests people's character, their faith, obedience, love, integrity and loyalty towards Him. Words, like trials and temptations occur more than 200 times in the Bible.

We see where God tested Abraham, by asking him to offer his son, Isaac. God tested Jacob when he had to work extra years to earn the hand of Rebecca. The Bible tells us of many others who endured trials and tribulations in their lives. But, the Bible also gives us many examples of people who passed the test of trials and tribulations, such as Joseph, Ruth, Esther and Daniel.

Unlike Job's wife in the Bible, I didn't ask my husband to curse God and die. I had to remind myself, that this could be me and I asked myself, how would I want to be treated? I like the golden rule. "Do unto others, as you would have them do unto you."

A friend said to me, "Child you need to tell your story and be an encouragement to some of us older women." She said, "What you're going through can't be easy and you need to tell us how you're surviving." She was right! It isn't easy to support a hurting spouse. One thing to realize is that none of the other responsibilities drop off, and now more is added. The family affairs still need to be taken care of, the children, the 8-hour job, and the church commitments etc. My personal agenda was put on the back burner for things that mean the most for him and his healing. I had to remember that when he gets better, it will be a better life for both of us.

Supporting a hurting spouse requires lots of love, patience, hope, understanding, communication and the right attitude.

I learned that his battle with Keloids was also my battle. His trial with Keloids was not all about him-it included me too. God has a purpose in this trial for me. I knew that God was looking at me to see how I was treating His child. I didn't want to flunk the test. Also, I knew that I had to be well grounded and rooted in the Word to be strong enough to be there for his support.

Thus, I would read the Bible, listen to gospel tapes, watch TV ministry, attend worship services, all to gather the support, encouragement and strength I needed. I did not want my faith to waver. I must tell you at times, my faith did waver. But, the Holy Spirit brought me back on course.

What I saw with my eyes, as I was preparing the deep wounds, was Lord how can he heal? The wounds were so deep. I will always remember the wounds and how they looked. I would continue to carefully put the bandages on while praying. We have to realize when something is too big for us we have to totally give it over to God. This was a job for God. More than once, the Holy Spirit had to remind me that I serve a God that is able and that there is nothing to big for Him.

As a spouse, I needed to be there for him emotionally, physically, and spiritually, not necessarily in that order.

How can you be a support to a hurting spouse? By applying the following spiritual values:

Love your spouse. Love has to be foremost the primary thing in supporting a hurting spouse, for without love Christ said we are like a sounding brass, just making noise (1 Corinthians 13:1). God expects us to love as He loves, unconditional love, not expecting anything in return.

Pray for your spouse. I prayed daily for his healing and that my husband would not loose faith in Christ and His power. Be careful for nothing but in everything by prayer and supplication with thanksgiving, let you requests be made known unto God.

Patient with your spouse. Roman 5:3 tells us that tribulation works patience.

Faith in Jesus Christ. You know what you see with your eyes but Hebrews 11:1 says, "without faith, it's impossible to please God."

Communicate with your spouse by asking, "What can I do for you?" Ask your spouse, "How can I be of service today?" I found myself trying to keep his bandages clean, have his meal ready on time, and all the other responsibilities that go with maintaining the household. By communicating with him I found that, at times, he just wanted me to sit and just be in his presence and stop being a busy body.

Encouragement is what your spouse needs for recovery. Remember that your spouse is depending on you to get him or her through the hurt. Go the extra mile to accomplish those things that speeds up the healing process.

Many would have given up on life if they had to endure what he has. I admire him for his courageous spirit, and for not letting society cause him to sit in a backroom somewhere and have a pity party. He didn't do that. He continued his regular work routine and never compromised doing what he wanted to do. I learned to respect my husband more for his inner strength, which he displayed during his time of trial. Also, I learned that my spouse is a very strong and courageous man with resilience. My love grew stronger for him and my faith increased as I watched God work through his life. He is now vibrant and energetic, doing activities I haven't witnessed him do in years.

To date, my spouse didn't let the Keloids take his faith, freedom or fight from him. In fact, the surgeries performed during the period of April through July 2003 have been 80% successful. The scarring after those seven surgeries has been 1,000 times less. His energy is back to its normal level. Most importantly, he has been led by God to write a book on what he experienced and how God kept him through his storm.

Some of you are facing trials and tribulations; it may be financial hardship, educational blockage, emotional depression, family member living ungodly lives, and ministerial frustration, health issues, or whatever. I am telling this story to be an encouragement to you. Have faith in God and trust Him for He already knows what you're going through and He alone knows the end results.

What's different about my story than any other woman's story? God allowed me to witness, experience and see a truly loving husband go through such a struggle and trial with the skin disorder, Keloids. The Keloids are so horrific that even doctors marvel after and report that they have not seen such large Keloids in their entire practice. God allowed my spouse to get through all the operations successfully, and for this he and I are so grateful to God. I thank God that he allowed me to have the strength to be there for him during his most severe struggle with Keloids. I know he wants me to share the story to be an encouragement to someone who is wondering how he or she will make it through the trial of supporting a hurting spouse. No one can tell my story. God gave this story to me.

FAITH IS THE KEY, GOD IS THE ANSWER

I hope that as you read this story that you have been inspired and encouraged.

(Note: All scriptural references are taken from the Ryrie Bible, Moody Press, Chicago.)

Quotes 7
By Lille' McGhee

"Don't hold onto anything in life that does not add positive value…"

"The grass is not greener on the other side of town-the secrets are in the soil."

"A Wedding Anniversary celebration is a moment of reflection, happiness and joy!"

No Way to Escape Love

By Lille' McGhee

Turbulence fills the
blue waters;
darkness covers the
deep sea, there is a lover
somewhere at shore
waiting to discover
me.

How will I know
where to look,
Once the ship is
no longer at sea?

Will a silent voice
direct me to
my lover;
the love that was
meant to be?

Three long days,
two empty nights
gone by; I'm left in a state
of worry.

I am in need of
love, this very

moment, so God,
"Why don't you
hurry?"

There is no way to
escape the beauty
of love,
so I'll close my
eyes once more.

The man in the
mirror at sea,
he's now waiting
for me at shore!

Running From, Running To
By Carolyn Jolly Douglas

Have you ever seen the walking dead? I bet you have, but were not aware of it. Let me give you an example of what I am talking about. But let me warn you first. This is a true story.

A few years ago, I lived a comfortable life in Tennessee surrounded by loving family and friends. My two sons and I had much to be grateful for. We had a lovely home, a late model car, and other material things to indicate that we were doing okay financially. Every day was pretty much the same and everything I did was like clockwork. Get up, make breakfast, get the kids to the babysitter and school, work eight hours, get the kids, go home, have dinner, then go to bed. Oh yeah, there were the Saturday outings to do shopping and fun stuff, church on Sunday, and then we returned to our regular weekly schedule.

Routines are good to have. I needed them to ensure that I got it all done. Besides, how could I be called a super mom if I didn't do all the things that society was saying made me a fulfilled modern day woman? You see, the roles for women inside and outside of the home were under scrutiny and being redefined. The definition of a liberated woman was being expressed in feminism through song, poetry, prose, and activism. In a nutshell, it said that I am an autonomous, sovereign individual able to make decisions for myself, that I am my own person, and I can have what I want. Thank you, Helen Redding, Gloria Steinem, Alice Walker, and Gloria Gaynor. Something is calling me to be more! Something is calling me to explore the possibilities! "I AM WOMAN! Hear me roar!"

Oops! That's another story. Let's return to the one about the zombie; you know, the walking dead.

If you have ever watched scary movies, you are likely to have seen a zombie-a creature that looks and behaves like an automaton or a robot. According to voodoo cult belief, it is basically a reanimated corpse that moves around in a trancelike state doing what it is commanded to do. Suffice it to say, the routine of my sedate, secure life made me feel zombie-like. Everything I did was performed perfunctory. I was on automatic pilot. I was the walking dead.

Imagine this. Here I am, an educated woman moving from day-to-day with no expectation of anything other than the ordinary, not even a vision of fifteen minutes of fame. Even the excitement of working in a research laboratory had dimmed to mediocrity. Was my contribution to this life to be limited to procreation and nurturing my children? Dorothy Height. Angela Davis. Somebody, help me. I love my children. I love my parents. But I want more. I want to feel the world. Will somebody call Dr. Frankenstein, please?

The realization of my state of being no longer fits me. I wear discontentment and restlessness on the surface of my skin. My existence is ready for shock. No more playing it safe. Do you hear that song? Diana Ross and the Supremes are singing. "I'm coming out. I want the world to know. I've got to let it show." I, Carolyn, am kissing the grave goodbye. No more dead person walking. Oh, I just heard Dr. Frankenstein scream. "She's alive. She's alive."

December 4, 1985 is known as the day I ran away from home. A few months earlier, I informed my family that I was moving across country. Initially, I was not taken seriously. However, as I took those giant steps to make the move happen, arguments, statements of disbelief and denial followed. "Why?" asked my mother. "Why do you have to go so far away? You are a woman, and you cannot drive all the way across country with those children." "You are crazy," added my brother. "This is the best place for you." No manner of explanation was good enough to convince them that I knew what I was doing. And, I could not allow their perceived limitations to dictate my life any longer.

Each morning I prayed for strength to keep my resolve. That's when I'd hear Gloria Gaynor singing, "I will survive". So, I shut my ears to what I did not want to hear and closed my eyes to what I did not want to see. I began the process of letting go of attachments and saying goodbye to people that I had known for a lifetime. I sold my house, gave away furniture and clothing. I explained to my young sons that we were about to start a new life. That meant that we would leave a lot of the things we were familiar with behind. They were excited and saw it as an adventure. So I made it one. We mapped out all the cool spots and landmarks to visit along the way.

As we left Tennessee, I began to breathe with relief. My new life was beginning. What laid ahead for me? It was both scary and exhilarating. I was launching out into the unknown with my children and I did not have an immediate safety net around me. Each day of our 5-day trip brought something new.

Within three years of arriving in California, my life changed drastically for the better. I went back to graduate school, switched careers, taught my sons to be excellent cooks and more independent. I work and live among people from different cultures and countries in the world. I teach others to enhance the quality of their lives through creativity and spirituality. Diversity fills my life. I pay close attention to what is going on around me because if I am not engaged, I may miss out on something wonderful. Not only do I share my life with others, I want to be a facilitator of something good existing for all humankind. My life is full of color. I am so alive.

Gifts of an Angel
By Linda Garrett

The wonderful person that you are,
The precious gifts that you share
To listen with care, leaving judgement behind
To give and love without conditions attached
To sacrifice one's self for the good of others
With a commitment and dedication to nurturing

The endless courage to face all obstacles
With faith and endurance, and the warmth of God's love
To stay on the path, despite loneliness or setbacks
To be determined to follow the sacred light

Following inner guidance, independent of others
With unlimited strength and wisdom
To truly see the beauty in all things
And to appreciate what is important in life

To follow the true journey of your soul
And to know in your heart it is for the highest
good of all
Is a precious gift that life has to offer

How fortunate are we all to be so incredibly blessed
By one who is filled with divine light
And touches our souls with magic and grace

Quotes 8
By Lille' McGhee

"The taller trees in the forest grow unevenly to protect the younger trees from potential harm."

"It is impossible for you to see all of my greatness in your lifetime…"

"You have the right to think very little of me-I have the right to ignore you."

Radiant Spirit

By Linda Garrett

You are an angel
That has come to bring
Light into the world

So generous and kind
With a radiant spirit
And sincere love for others

You have blessed my life
With your divine presence
And sacred love

To know you is to see
Strength and courage
Inspiring everyone that you touch
with your magic

The power of your light is endless
You reveal the truth and faith
That the power of love creates miracles

The Clock is . . .T.I.C.K.I.N.G.
By Lille′ McGhee

As we all grow older,
They say, "Life takes on a different
Pace;
Less multi-tasking,
Stressing out,
AND
Rushing to
Be in first place."

We have ALL been there

We have ALL done that

When all of THAT

Mattered most

It is exciting
TODAY, in
Looking back at
YESTERDAY, and asking,
"Where did the time go?"

There is no better time
Than now
My friend,

Lille' McGhee-Queen

To start sharing everything
YOU know,
BY helping ONE
Homeless family,
Disabled child,
Blind man crossing
the street,
Then watching their
Faces glow…

SO,
Take a walk in
A rose garden
TODAY, and
Pick Just
One Yellow Rose;
'CAUSE

The "Clock is ticking"
My friend, BUT
Who is watching the clock?

I'm not.

The "Clock is ticking"
My friend, BUT
Who is listening,

I'm not.

Nobody Wants To Go Home!

Contributors

Dr. Sherezad F. Czar is multi-tasked, multi-disciplinary, and multi-talented.

As a doctor, he authored, Around the Waist in 80 Days, in 1998, which ultimately has become his core weight loss philosophy. A jury of over 100 doctors declared it as the "Easiest Weight Loss Program in the World". His approach to obesity management is the closest as one can get in terms of human physiology and biochemistry.

He is an ambidextrous, gifted calligrapher and will soon be launching a project to scribe Bible in English, Koran in Arabic, and Torah in Hebrew. The proceeds from this project named, "Signature America", will contribute directly to Nuzhat Czar Cancer Endowment Fund.

His lifetime work is, Dr.Czar's Business Encyclopedia, which lists approximately half-a-million copyright business models, which he has to his name. It also makes him a man with most copyrights in the world.

His office is located at 1131 New Park Mall, Newark, CA 94536. Phone: 510-405-1807. Cell: 510-396-3779 E-mail: dr.czar@sbcglobal.net and drsfczar@hotmail.com.

Frederico Domondon was born in Manila, Philippines in July 1964. In August 1980, he migrated to the United States when his mother married an American lawyer. In the fall of 1989, Frederico graduated with an accounting degree from San Francisco State University. Ten years later, he quit his accounting job to follow his dream of becoming a full-time artist. In addition to being an artist, in 2003 he became a professional pianist and vocalist.

He can be reached at www.domondon.com, (415) 640-1657, or by E-mail: frederico@domondon.com.

Carolyn Jolly Douglas is a teacher, spiritual counselor, and community builder. She has several years experience working with state, local and tribal governments in program development, and is adept at looking at the big picture, strategic planning, and communications to achieve programmatic objectives and goals.

Her educational disciplines integrate science, management, and spirituality. Her commitment to service and life includes mentoring students and servicing her spiritual community.

She currently resides in Northern California and can be reached at caroldoug@comcast.net.

Linda Garrett has always had a love for the arts. She enjoyed writing poetry, playing music, performing dance and creating art.

In addition to working as an artist and writer, Linda is also a part-time Landscape Architect having acquired her bachelor's degree from University of California at Davis in 1989. In 1998 she was moved to pursue her passion and become a professional artist, specializing in inspirational art and writing.

Her loving relationships, her passion for life and her ongoing self-discovery and expansion inspires Linda Garrett's creations. Her vision is to inspire the minds, elevate the spirits and warm the hearts of people around the world. Her work is a reminder that each of us has the ability to create miracles through the power of love and inspiration.

Linda Garrett Creations: Inspirational Art and Writing, P.O. Box 23073, San Jose, CA 95153, (408) 365-2075 Lgarrett@bat-net.com www.lindagarrett.com

Anna Griffin was raised in Vicksburg, Mississippi, but now resides in Northern California. She enjoys family life, storytelling and business ventures.

Her most fulfilling and rewarding activity is teaching young children in Sunday school. "Stillness" in Vicksburg, Mississippi is a quiet reflection of early childhood memories of her parent's love for recreation and solitude.

Creating a quiet place where people can come to transform their harried lives through meditation and learning how to savor the pleasures and joys of living is her highest business aspiration. E-mail: annamar1@juno.com

Varek Queen was born in Tacoma Park, MD but has spent all of his adult life in Northern California.

His essay for his tenth-grade class assignment entitled, *An Unfinished Masterpiece*, highlights his life as a teenager in transition.

After graduating from High School in Maryland, June 1989, he went directly into the U.S. Army, and returned to California in 1991. He attended The National Hispanic University, majored in Business Administration, and currently holds a professional position in the Gaming Industry.

He is single, enjoys writing short stories/quotes, and spending time with his son and their dog.

He can be reached at lillebooks@hotmail.com.

Joyce Sherman is a native of Mobile, AL. She and her family reside in Northern California.

A licensed financial analyst and an accredited Public Purchasing Practitioner, she also holds a Bachelor of Arts Degree in Business Management from California State University, Bakersfield.

She services in several church capacities as Director of Sunday School, Sunday School Teacher, Vacation Bible School Teacher, and Chairperson of the Usher Board.

Her story, How to Support a Hurting Spouse, is spiritually compelling.

She can be reached at Face-to-Face Ministries, 1-800-858-7314 (pass code #25), FAX (408) 730-1322.

Angela S. Woods was born in Roxboro, NC and grew up in Greensboro, NC. She graduated from James B. Dudley Senior High School and after two years of college she joined the United States Navy.

After extensive travel and seventeen years of service, she retired "Honorably" from the United States Navy in October 1995.

She now lives in Greensboro, North Carolina with her three children.

You can reach her at angelagreensboro@aol.com.

About the Author

Lille' McGhee-Queen is a retired Federal Investigator who continues to get involved in many businesses, professional and fun projects, such as storytelling, business lecturer, keynote public speaker, business owner, author, poet, artist, pianist, and writer.

She currently resides in Northern California with her spouse, Mike Queen. They have one son and one grandson. Publications to her credit include: Self-Published - Handbook of Procedures for the Immigration Courtroom 1978; Article - Prep Before Plunging, Wall Street Journal, The National Business Employment Weekly Newspaper, 1987; Article - Career Transitions: Prep Before Plunging Into New Careers, The Washington Living Magazine, (May 1987) and (June 1987); Self-Published - WORKBOOK: Job Interview Savvy II (Tough Questions & Appropriate Answers), (Revised) 1993; and Poem, Marriage in a Small Town - The Lightness of Being, The International Library of Poetry, 2002.

Educational Credits: Associate of Arts Degree in Court & Conference Reporting, Strayer College, Washington, D.C., Bachelor of Science Degree in Human Relations & Organizational Behavior, University of San Francisco, San Francisco, CA; Graduate Program, University of San Francisco

Lille', and some of the co-authors, are available to conduct business seminars, storytelling hour, poetry readings, workshops, art exhibits (paintings), and live musical performances.

Contact her at McGhee, Queen & Associates, P.O. Box 360-823, Milpitas, CA 95036; E-mail: lillebooks@hotmail.com and lillemcghee@hotmail.com

Comments & Ordering Information

We would like to hear from you. If you have comments or suggestions, or would like to order additional copies of *Every Woman Has a Short Story, Men Too!*, please contact us: lillebooks@hotmail.com or www.jirehpublishing.com.

There are several ways to place your order.

For additional copies of this book, send check or money order in the amount of $19.95 per copy (includes shipping & handling and tax), with Ordering Information form.

Make payable to:

MC GHEE, QUEEN & ASSOCIATES
c/o: Lille' McGhee-Queen
P.O. Box 360-823
Milpitas, CA 95036
E-mail: lillebooks@hotmail.com

COMPLETE ORDER FORM

(Please Print)

Name _____

Address _____

State _____ Zip Code _____

Telephone: (   ) _____

Business phone: (   ) _____

____ copies of *Every Woman Has a Short Story, Men Too!* @ $19.95 per copy (includes S/H & taxes)

Total Amount Enclosed: $_____

Checks/Money Orders Payable to:

MC GHEE, QUEEN & ASSOCIATES
c/o: Lille' McGhee-Queen
P.O. Box 360-823
Milpitas, CA 95036
E-mail: lillebooks@hotmail.com

NOTES

NOTES

NOTES

NOTES

NOTES

NOTES

NOTES

NOTES

NOTES

NOTES

NOTES

NOTES